BEYOND

The Bead and I

by Marla L. Gassner

Complete instructions
for making 25 original
and unforgettable pieces
of beaded jewelry.

To Marilyn —
Bead on —
Regards,
Marla Louise Gassner

Inquires addressed to:
Marla L. Gassner
213 Woodstone Drive, Buffalo Grove, Illinois 60089-6703
(847) 541-1910 or MGAS726@cs.com

The Library of Congress Control Number: 2001127190

Gassner, Marla L.
　　Beyond the Bead and I: complete instructions for 25 original and unforgettable pieces of beaded jewelry / by Marla L. Gassner. -- 1st ed.
　　p. cm.
　　ISBN: 0-9661236-3-8

　　1. Beadwork.　2. Jewelry making.　I. Title.

Printed in China
by Regent Publishing Services, Ltd.

**To my students
who loved the first book
and asked for more
and my friends
who encouraged me to write it.**

ACKNOWLEDGMENTS

I always envision the biggest dream because it keeps me excited and that excitement is infectious. It carries me along as well as the people I infect, until we turn it into reality. For a woman who is independent, and sometimes obstinate, it is difficult for me to ask for help.

This second book, has turned out to be substantially larger and more involved that the first one. While I had more experience, I had far less help. I was most fortunate that the writing of it came easily to me and once having accomplished this there was no turning back. There are complete instructions for twenty-one advanced and unique projects including the two intricate necklaces on my picture postcard and the original four introductory, learning projects, for a grand total of twenty-five projects. I wanted to give you everything! Therefore, I stretched myself to do it or prevailed on the "right" people to ensure this would be the best and most complete book possible.

I wish first to acknowledge the creative process, in the same way that I say. "thank you for yesterday, thank you for today" to the Universe, when I stand in my shower each morning. Even if yesterday was a disaster or today promises to be filled with difficult challenges, saying "thank you" has become my way of acknowledging that what comes into my life will be examined and integrated in the most creative way possible. That the synchronicity of the Universe brings help to my work when I open my eyes, mind and heart to it. That if my enthusiasm for what I do and want to accomplish is sincere I can engage other like-minded people to aid me. Therefore, I wish to thank those people who have helped me make this book a reality.

To America Martinez, The Universe first brought me to America about eight years ago, but it was only after my first book "The Bead and I" went out into the world that I realize how important her very first psychic message had been for me to hear. On that day, eight years ago, she knew and channeled the message that the Universe wanted me to know. Since that day I have come to accept and believe that the writing is an important part of my life and destiny. America, made me aware of this and encouraged me to validate my voice. For this awakening and for her continued encouragement I wish to thank her. If there are angels meant to speak to us in an earthly manner, certainly America is one of them and I am fortunate that we were brought together.

To Karen Flowers, who was willing to do even more diagrams that she did for the first book, I wish to acknowledge the beauty and detail of her work. She is truly an artist, in every sense of the word and one of the few people whose talents and opinions I have come to value and respect. This book would not be half so beautiful or successful without her interpretations of my stick drawings and her love for me. Thank you.

To Terri Brown, who I first met when she was my roommate at an Embellishment Conference six years ago. We bonded instantly, staying up late, exchanging stories and jokes as we tried to unwind after the days we spent teaching, before sleep would come. Her professional expertise as an artist and teacher, combined with her attention to detail have kept me looking and sounding correct. We do not get to spend very much time together now and converse via Email, but it is always like coming home to a good friend. Thank you for your friendship and your help with all things technical.

To Sybil Virshbo, thank you for the time you spent proof reading all the non-technical parts of this manuscript. You taught me that I could begin sentences with "ands" and "buts" and tidied up all my rambling words. You also encouraged me to keep up my work on this book.

To Tom Van Endye, my photographer, who made it easy to get the photographs that I needed to make a beautiful book, thank you. This proves that two creative Aquarians can work well together!

To my friends, Rachel Jacobsohn, and Valerie Gorelick, who have both insisted on writing a comment about me to be included on the back of this book, I thank you. Your encouragement and willingness to hear every ongoing detail of this project is proof of the best kind of friendship and I am most fortunate to have it.

To my friend, Marla Skolnik, who when I had a panic attack before I was about to go off to teach in July at Embellishments and the book was in a very vulnerable state, I asked to oversee the making of it, if something were to happen to me; and she said "Yes". She is the only one I know who has the time and artistic experience and judgment to have put together all the pieces to make this book. Her willingness to have possibly taken on such a project in my behalf is truly the gesture of a loving friend and I thank her for it.

To my daughters, Suzanne Gassner and Jennifer Gassner Mc Daniel, who are both teachers and writers, distinguished in their own names, it is joyous for me to be able to share such gifts and talents with both of you. I hope living my life openly and to the fullest; accomplishing some of my fondest dreams and goals will encourage you both to do the same. Thank you for reading my precious words and knowing how important they are to me.

To Barbara Lopez, who in the process of helping with my last book, found herself a wonderful husband and now lives in Pittsburgh. I wish to thank you ahead of time for hopefully being able to coordinate the checking of my color proofs for this book with you in-between your bi-annual business trips to India. If we are successful in connecting, I know I can count on your printing expertise and good advise on whatever might need to be done. Thank you.

To Phyllis Kaplan, who worked wonders on the computer that I never knew existed. She managed to fit every diagram into the correct place, with its words and put together all the wonderful colors on the cover design. She did it in a pleasant and timely manner and it really helped that she had bead knowledge, as well. Thank you for your very professional work, attitude and observing all my deadlines.

To my sister, Lauren Goldberg, who has dubbed me the "writer" of the family. Her feisty, fire-sign personality helps me stay excited and brings new things into my life. If I move out to Phoenix, which I am contemplating, it will in part be due to my sister's urging and the expectation of sharing a new adventure with her and beading experiences with west coast beaders.

TABLE OF CONTENTS

INTRODUCTION FOR BEYOND THE BEAD AND I

Now, I am always thinking about writing. One evening eight years ago I was taken to a psychic by a student of mine. I was open to this reading because on previous occasions I had learned a great deal. You see, I never sought this kind of information out on my own and only went along when I trusted a friend's judgement, so that in itself was a kind of endorsement.

I have even come to believe that when we are truly searching for answers, psychics are channelers for the correct thoughts and ideas coming in from the universe. So on this particular evening, the psychic I saw completely changed my perception of writing. Her message was more than clear, it was succinct, even emphatic....she told me that I was meant to write and while the jewelry I created was beautiful, it was the writing I would do which I would become known for. This was long before I even thought of writing The Bead and I.

I was not altogether surprised by what this psychic said, because I have always written. Journalling in spiral notebooks, tearing away the first drafts as I revised my thoughts into more and more perfect forms, has long been a habit of mine. I asked the psychic what I should write about since my writing began for the sole reason of dissipating the emotional pain of a traumatic childhood. Later I wrote to define the questions that were always in my head, to document my observations and possible answers.

I had considered my writing a waste product, in the same way one might vomit when they had the flu, as a cleansing, thus enabling me to dissipate the emotional pain and move on. I told this to the physic, I was not surprised by her noticing in her cards that I wrote. No, she exclaimed, *"the writing is not a discard.....it is the product, it is what you are meant to do; what you will be known for and what will remain."*

This was a revelation to me and I began to think of myself as a writer. She suggested that I start by writing my own autobiography. Nine months later, I had written ninety-five typed pages chronicling my life from birth to the age of nineteen. In the refining of that story I realized things about my parents I had never seen before. It was an epiphany for me as well as a great writing exercise.

Writing is very different from remembering. We think we know the story, but when we literally have to put the words down on the page choosing each and every verb, adverb, adjective and noun; then this process becomes far more deliberate. In fact, it is radically different than merely telling ourselves a story.

Since that psychic reading, I have thought much more seriously about writing. I started writing a philosophy book based on special words, words that have fascinated me throughout my life. Alphabetically, I list the words and then I write a personal essay about each of them. To date, there are some thirty-five finished essays, and over one hundred words on my list. This book is still unfinished. I want this book to document the middle of my life: what I feel about where I am now. If nothing else comes of it, my daughters and their children will never have to wonder what I might have thought about these things or ideas. The working title of this book is "One Woman's Words". I also have over two thousand poems about love and nature that I hope to put into a more permanent form.

In the interim, I wrote "The Bead and I." That was in 1996. Two things made me write that book: first, to verify that the work of my hands was original; and second, my need to let go of these ideas, and move on to new things. Life and love are about *letting go,* I audaciously sent my creation out into the Universe.

When I think back on it, the idea of writing, publishing and marketing my own book still scares me. Yet, when I started writing it flowed out of me in six short weeks while I was recovering from pneumonia. This showed me how fully developed and natural it was for me to write it down. What happened during the next year is a book in itself. The Universe wanted this book to be made and shared, and brought all sorts of people and money to publish it to my aid. There were even a few who tried to foil me, yet the book took on a life of its own.

I only began to be nervous when I realized I had stuck myself out there for possibly the worst kind of criticism by my fellow beadworkers. What boldness, new techniques, new supplies, new uses for old or found objects! I had even made the stringing easier. But that has not been the case, from the start the biggest distributor in this field wanted to distribute my book and talked me into a deal I have repeatedly thanked him for making. Bead societies and bead stores across the country, in places I never knew of, are selling my book. I have a filing cabinet drawer full of emails and personal notes from beaders, both experienced and novices, from every corner of this country telling me how much they like my book.

Whenever I go out to teach and lecture "The Bead and I" is with me because you, the readers and students, have asked for it. It is all of you that make it clear to me I have done the right thing by writing "The Bead and I". It is for this very reason that I have written this new book....BEYOND, THE BEAD AND I. You have asked for more and I have more to give.

If my books afford me any immortality, I hope it will be in the joy students will derive in reading and using them. Therefore, I dedicate this book to you, my students and to my friends who encouraged me to keep creating with beads and with words.

BEFORE YOU BEGIN TO USE THIS BOOK

With a few hundred copies of the original first book left, I decided I would write a new book which starts with the original four projects so each book would stand alone. I will then take you on to new advanced projects. If you are familiar with the basics, skip over them or refresh your bead muscle memory by doing them again. Then go on to the new advanced projects that I know you will find as exciting as I do.

I see that the world of beading is divided into off-loom beaders, who are seed beaders, and bead stringers who remain on the low part of the totem pole of beading. Why, I don't know? As it is just as difficult to conceive and execute an intricate strung piece of jewelry as it is any off loom piece. The truest test should be, is it good design, good color and proper proportion?

Personally, I am a stringer and proud of it. In fact, I might be one of the great stringers! I make a good portion of my living from designing one of a kind pieces of jewelry. I seriously doubt that I would have entertained such an idea if I had not found and successfully been able to use fishline. It would not have been time/cost effective. In fact, my discovery and experimentation with this product changed the entire direction of my career.

Stringing is something I do the better part of most of my days. I still love it and find new and different things that inspire me. Perhaps not every beadworker will become a bead artist but every beadworker can learn to make beautiful, wearable, sophisticated jewelry using my books.

Please read all the non-technical parts of this book first. Then read each project from start to finish before you begin to do it. Also look carefully at the gallery in the back of the book and to see variations of some of the projects.

The reason the margins in this book are so wide is to allow you the space to make your own notes or drawings. In addition there are a few blank pages for the same reason.

Supplies for First Four Projects

The following is the list of supplies that you will need to do the first four learning or introductory projects:

1   10 o round seed beads

2   6 o or "E" beads to match the color of the seed beads

3   A pair of small sharp scissors

4   1 roll of 12lb. fish line (preferably see-though blue)

5   1 tube of crazy glue

6   1 tube of E 6000 glue

7   Assortment of "fancy" beads as diagrammed to match your color schemes and in various sizes.

8   1 knotting board at least 1/2 inch thick that will hold T-pins tightly

9   6 T-pins or wig pins

10 1 roll of conso size 18 in beige, taupe or black to match your color palette (one roll will do every project in this book 2 or 3 times).

11 3 pairs of pliers...flat and needle nose and cutting (these tools are not used very much. Perhaps you can borrow them, but if you buy them, buy good ones).

12 2 or more clams or bead tips

13 2 or more Shepard hooks or French earring wires

14 1 button: 1 1/2 inches or more in diameter with metal shank back

15 1, 1inch or 1 1/2 inch pin back that can be glued'

You can still order all the beading supplies for the first four projects, including fish line, knotting board and T-pins for the price of $85 plus S&H of $5, for a grand total of $90. Find mailing address in the back of the book.

As still available from the first book "The Bead and I" are these kits:

1   Tutti-Fruitti, Carmen Miranda Bracelet $34
2   The Great Rope Trick Lariat $48
3   The Antique Button Bracelet $42

All kits come in several color combinations and includes all supplies needed.

The advanced projects in this book are meant to be one of a kind, therefore it is really up to you to find the proper, components and supplies.

I have tried to give you as much current information as I possibly could to direct you to the persons or places for specialized supplies. This data is listened in each individual project.

I do stock some of the elements and supplies, as well as a few projects that can be made up into kits. I will list these with my current prices, which are subject to possible price changes and availability.

1	Roll of 12lb. blue beading monofilament, 375 yds.	$ 4
2	Roll of Conso cord #18 in 10 basic colors.	$ 8
3	Brown iris seed beads on strings by the hank.	$ 5
4	Brown iris "E" Beads, in tubes or small bags.	$ 2.50
5	Various "fancy" beads, seeds, and "E" beads individually priced	
6	The stick with 25 drilled holes for the **Stick Necklace,** #10.	$20

KITS: Which include all necessary supplies

1	**Any Bead into a Beaded Tassel**, several color schemes, #16.	$35
2	**Freeform Found Object Pin**, faces or minerals, #12.	$24

Please keep in mind, that these prices do not include shipping or handling.

Speak with Marla for any specific or further information, call: (847) 541-1910

Email: MGas726@cs.com

"Fancy Beads"

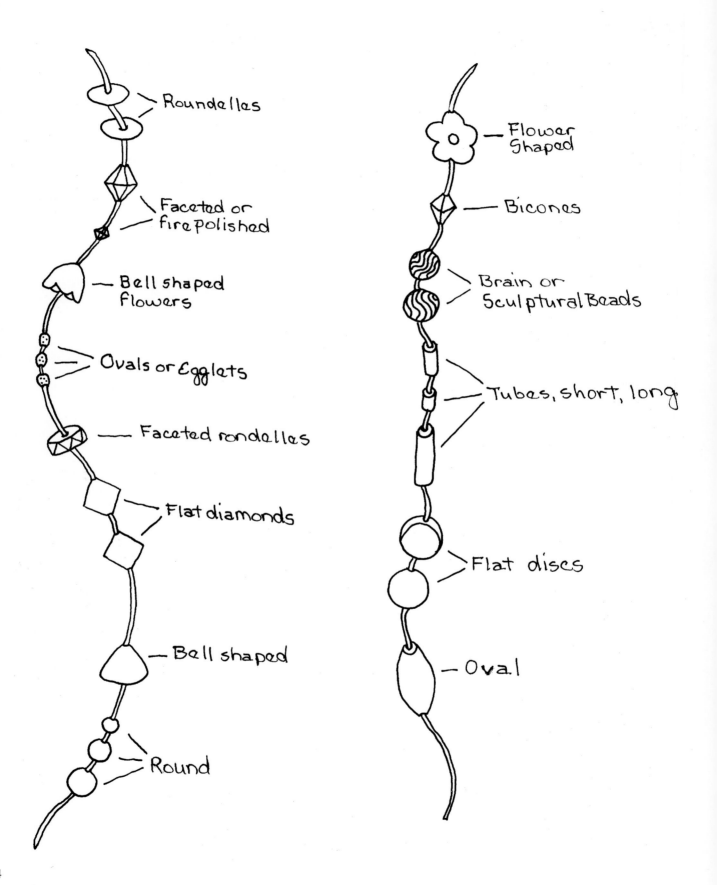

Roundelles

Faceted or fire polished

Bell shaped Flowers

Ovals or Egglets

Faceted rondelles

Flat diamonds

Bell shaped

Round

Flower Shaped

Bicones

Brain or Sculptural Beads

Tubes, short, long

Flat discs

Oval

SO LET'S START!

The first thing we will do is learn to knot between beads. There are three reasons why learning to knot between beads is important.

1. Knots delineate each bead by separating one from another

2. If your beads should break you will not lose all of them.

3. When you knot between beads your total length increases, therefore, if you have a short strand, say 12 inches of grandmother's beads, when you knot between them the extended length will be eighteen inches, or up to 1/2 again the original length.

KNOTTING: A PRACTICE EXERCISE

Supplies

- 1 1/2 yards (or the measurement from your hand to your shoulder and your hand to your elbow, which is equivalent) of Conso 3-ply waxed nylon size #18.

- 20 medium size glass beads in a bright color that is easy to see on the color of your Conso cord.

Step-by-Step Instructions

1   Make an overhand knot at the end of your length of Conso cord, as if you were making a knot at the end of sewing thread.

2   Cut the opposite end on an angle against your finger to make a sharp angle or point at the end of it. See diagram. This will enable you to string the beads on easily because of the wax.

3   Put your first bead on the Conso cord letting it fall to the knotted end. Make a lasso of the remaining cord and manipulate that circle, reeling it in to get it as tight and as close as possible to the bead. Repeat with the next bead. Keep practicing knotting with the next 20 beads, placing them as close as possible to one another. If they are further apart do not bother taking a knot out. Just keep going, eventually your muscle memory will kick in and you will get better at this. Don't be afraid to manipulate the loop. When you have knotted all these beads on your cord then cut them off and knot them again. If you have 2 colors of Conso cord then change the color of the cord the 2nd time you knot. The necklace you are about to make calls for precision knotting . . . so practice and then go one to the 1st project: the Floating Fantasy Necklace.

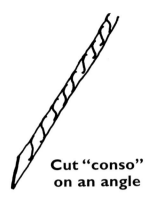

Cut "conso" on an angle

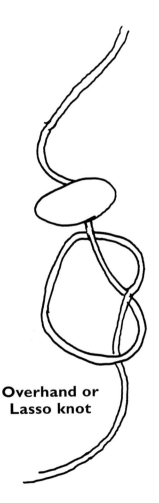

Overhand or Lasso knot

SECTION I BEGIN AGAIN

PROJECT I
FLOATING FANTASY NECKLACE

Supplies

- Conso waxed nylon # 18
- Choose 24 small beads (4mm), 16 medium beads (6mm), and 8 large beads (8mm) and 200 "E" beads These beads should relate to each other as well as the color of the conso cord. (Get a few extra of each of your beads to use as decoration on the ends of your braid or else you can just use "E's". There are 16 ends.)
- Knotting Board, a 12x12 board made out of pressed or fiber board 1/2 inch thick that can hold T-pins tightly.
- 3 or 4 T-pins or wig pins

Step-by-Step Instructions

Before you begin your necklace cut 2 very long lengths of thicker yarn in 2 different colors, make an overhand knot using both at one end to hold them together and practice "Marla's braid". The color on the right always goes back to the right side after every knot, the color on the left always goes back to the left side after every knot, the side that is being knotted on remains "passive" or inactive and the side that is doing the knotting is "active" or moving. Tighten after every knot. If you do this knot correctly it should look like rick-rack. Try it again with 2 long lengths of conso knotted together in the middle and pin at the knot to the board...this will allow you to use the correct material and see how it feels to be knotting with 2 cords on each side and in each hand. (In class, we do both these exercises before we start the actual necklace). When you learn this braid you will find wonderful ways to incorporate it into your work and it is also part of the Antique Button Bracelet, at the end of this book, so get it down pat now, you will be glad you did. See diagram.

1 Using #18 Conso cord, measure 8 strands, each 3 yards in length.

2 Measuring backwards from either end, make an overhand knot at 25 inches, using all 8 cords together. Pin the knot down tightly to the knotting board with T-pins. (The shorter lengths should be coming down the front of the board, the longer lengths should be going over the top and under the back of the board so you won't be confused.)

3 Starting at the knot, pick up 4 of your 8 cords in each hand, working toward the short end do "Marla's braid". Technically, this is 1/2 of a double half hitch, this is a macramé term.) Stop 4 inches from the end of the cords. Pin the cords down to the board every few inches so you are not doing this braid up in the air.

**"Marla" braid
done loosely**

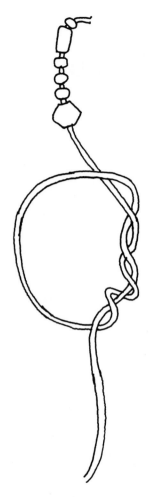

Beetle knot:

**An overhand knot
with the tail put
threw the hole
3 times or more,
then pull the end
to tighten.**

4 Now we are going to work the opposite or longer lengths of the cords. Using just 1 of your longer 8 cords, start knotting each of the beads you have selected for each individual strand. You are coming out of the corner where your big overhand knot is so you want to start with very small beads here so there is not a big jumble packed into the overhand knot. Here is how you know which beads go on each strand: (this design is based on 8 strands and the number of beads you selected are all divisible by that number. Therefore, each strand has 1 large bead, 2 medium beads, and 3 smaller beads, everything else or those beads in-between the others are "E" beads.)

5 Knot on each side of each bead individually, this holds the bead *exactly in place*, with the exception of the "E's" which you can string on 2 or 3 at a time (knotted on either side of them). *Leave no less that 1/4 inch and no more that 1 inch of empty cord between beads.* String until the strand measures 18 inches from your overhand knot, including your spaces; then leave the rest of the cord blank or empty. Vary the placement, sizes and shapes of your beads on each strand. See picture.

6 When all 8 cords have been individually knotted with their proper beads to the proper length gather them all up and adjust your strands slightly so they lie in a pleasing way and then make an overhand knot using all 8 cords like the one opposite your beads. Now do "Marla's Braid" from this knot down to 4 inches from the ends of cords or to the same length as the cord you braided on the opposite side.

7 Finish both ends with an overhand knot of all cords at the ends of the braid. Pull each individual strand of the knot to tighten it.

8 Decorate the ends with your extra beads or use various numbers of your "E" beads on each end. Let the beads dangle down from knot. Vary lengths slightly. Snip ends on an angle under knot, leaving about a 1/4 inch tail. See colored picture. Hold your beads on the cord with a "beetle" knot. See diagram.

This project should take about 6-8 hours to complete. It is a great thing to do in front of the T.V.

ADVICE AND VARIATIONS:

The colors you chose for your beads can be monochromatic or complimentary, matching or different from the color of the cord. If you should want to make a lot of these (students either love them or hate them) it is a good way to use up beads you already have or left-over beads. Start with a roll of Conso cord in either black or beige, these colors will go with almost any beads. Some of my students did all bright colored beads on black cord and it was very effective. Some made extra long bead dangles on the ends, but you must plan for this in the beginning so make you cords longer than 3 yards, maybe 4 yards and measure in further from the end for your overhand knot of all cords, maybe 30 inches. Do "Marla's Braid" for 8-10 inches and then leave the longer unknotted cords to dangle your beads from. If you are making your own kit, check the supply list carefully, chose different sizes and shape beads to make it more interesting. P.S. I do sell rolls of Conso #18 cord by the roll in about 10 colors.

MARLA'S SECRET WEAPON

Fish line. Yes, pure unadulterated fish line. It has gotten a really bad rap in the past, but don't believe everything you hear. My entire reputation as a designer of beaded jewelry is predicated on my use of fish line. People might tell you it stretches; it cracks or it breaks. Well, I am here to tell you that I make over two hundred original pieces of beaded jewelry a year using fish line. The fact is that I have pieces that I take with me as examples when I teach that are fifteen to eighteen years old and are still in good condition. My jewelry has been sold at the finest boutiques and stores in and around Chicago for the last twenty five years and I have had less than a 1% repair.

More often it is the person who is careless, not the way a piece of jewelry is made. I know this because my experience is that the same person breaks a piece of jewelry more than once. Beaded jewelry must be taken care of in certain ways. First, do not bunch it up in plastic bags; this will ruin it no matter what it is strung on. Instead hang it on a wall, lay it along the front of a draw lengthwise, keeping it as long as possible. Even hang it on door knobs. I hang mine on the wall on an antique hat rack. Do not wash with it on or spray perfume on it. Do not wear it to sleep or when you are planning to have sex. Do not wear it on the day you fly to Europe.... pack it! Pack handmade beaded jewelry by rolling it lengthwise in tissue paper. Pack it tightly so it won't roll around. Put it in the back or front of your suitcase or carry-on bag. If I am taking enough pieces I put them in a narrow bag such as the one they sell wine bottles in, so it doesn't move. You can make a roll or use the same kind holder used for needlepoint yarns. The idea is to keep it stretched out and not let it move around.

So where were we? Oh yes, fish line. The blue stuff you buy on a roll at a discount or sporting goods store. It runs about $1.47 to $2.98 depending on the number of yards on the roll; usually as little as 250 yards or as much as 700 yards. Now here is the magic number, the one not to forget: **12 pound test weight.** That means you can catch a 25 pound fish! Fish line comes in clear and blue. I

prefer blue because I can see it but no one else can once it is strung in a bead, even a clear crystal bead. I have tried every weight of fish line from 6 lb. to 20 lb. . . . 12 is the magic number. I cannot break it with my hands and it is still small enough to go through 12 o seed beads. You need not trust me. Experiment for yourself. However I could have included here the testimony of dozens and dozens of students who use my methods. Please, spend the remaining time fine tuning your skills by making all the wonderful projects I have outlined in this book and decide for yourself.

LET'S TRY SEED BEADS

Why do I love seed beads? Because seed beads are relatively inexpensive. Because they come in wonderful colors and finishes. Seed beads are round, with or without facets. Seed beads come on hanks; usually there are 10 or 12 hanks in a 1/2 kilo. There are 12 strands or loops in a hank. A strand or loop is usually about 16 inches long. I almost exclusively buy, use and sell Czechoslovakian glass beads and seed beads. Until you are skilled in the use of seed beads I would prefer that you use 10 o round seed beads, they can be "trusted" as I have already explained. Round beads are much more even in size and shape so that you can merely count as you work and the lengths come out even; you don't have to measure. My signature bead is Brown Iris, round, 10 o seeds, that I work in conjunction with "E" beads of the same color. In most cases, I use only several size seed beads: 6 oor "E", 10 o, no smaller than 12 o, and sometimes as big as a 8 o (in beads: the larger the number, the smaller the size of the bead).

Finishes: Iridescent, pearlized, silverlined, lined in different colors then the outside color.

Shapes: Round, 2 cut, 3 cut.

PROJECT 2
CONTINUOUS CRYSTAL ROPE

Supplies

- 4 strands or loops of 10 o seed beads
- "E" beads to match the color of your seeds (count 100)
- 1 roll of 12lb.weight (blue) fish line
- Assorted larger "fancy" beads to match or compliment your colors (see drawings and section on what to know to use the book).

Step-by-Step Instructions

1   Tie a knot in the end strings of all your seed bead loops or hank so they won't pull out.

2   Cut any one string of any loop holding it in one hand and take the your fish line about a needle's length away from the end in your other hand, and then put the cut end of the fish line up into and through the beads on the string as far as you can.

Now both are in the beads. Carefully transfer the beads from the string to the fish line, by pulling the fish line off the string the beads are on. (don't worry if you drop some) See numbered diagram on facing page.

3   Keep putting on seed beads and then stop and put on a "fancy" bead, or put 2 or 3 together (a bead "story") spaced out with seed beads between them. I string all seed bead strands at random, meaning with no set design. This is supposed to be fun! (See picture).

4   Follow the diagrams carefully; now you are going to learn to make a "bridge". A "bridge" allows you to keep your string taut while transferring seed beads and this is easier and faster. While holding the strand in your left or opposite hand between the thumb and forefinger, catch the string with the 3rd finger of your other hand. Then slide your fish line end across the string or "bridge" and into the line of beads. I know this sounds difficult, but after awhile it will become second nature and you won't even have to think about it. If you make a tight knot in the exposed thread you can then cut your strand away from the hank. This makes it faster and easier to transfer the seed beads.

ON THE LIFE LINE

To stop in your stringing, end with seed beads, tie a double knot near the very end of the fish line (one knot on top of the other). Then let your seeds drop down to the knot and roll up all the beads that you have just strung right on the roll of fish line. When you are ready to begin again, unroll and then cut the knot off at the end of the fish line and start stringing again. When you have strung on 3 loops of seed beads

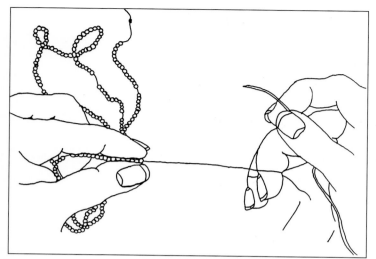

1 Setting up the bridge on 3rd finger of right hand, fish line held with thumb and forefinger and seed beads held between thumb and forefinger of left hand.

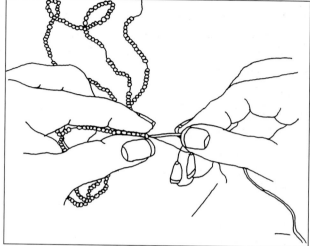

2 Following across the bridge with the fish line and into seed beeds.

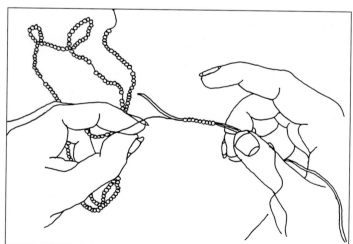

3 Push beads over off of string and onto fish line.

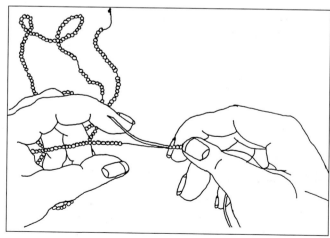

4 Seed beads now on fish line and pull fish line off of the string.

interspersed with all the "fancy" beads you want to add, you should have a measurement of 62-64 inches.

5 In preparation for ending, leave 6-8 inches of fish line on either side (that extends beyond the beads) then cut your bead work off the roll of fish line.

6 Keep the beads on the table, otherwise the weight will pull them out of your hands, smooth the beads down the fish line from both sides to be sure there are no gaps or empty line.

7 Add 2 "E" beads to each side and tie a 1/2 knot in the fish line up in the air above the beads, then a 2nd knot. As you tie the second 1/2 knot and pull all will tighten up. Tie a third 1/2 knot . . . now you have one square knot, (2 ties), and a 1/2 knot (1 tie), or three 1/2 knots in all.

8 These knots should go down inside between the "E" beads, they have bigger holes. Now, going backwards, coming from the middle triple knot, string your fish line ends down each side, through the big beads again until you have gone back through some of the seed beads and then pull your ends out. Do this on both sides with each end of the fish line going backwards through each side of the necklace, out from the central knot.

9 When all your work is done put a dot of Crazy Glue on the original knots in the middle of the "E" beads and cut away the ends of the fish line that are protruding out from the seed beads on either side. Cut flush or as close as possible (pull the fish line as you cut to get as close as possible.) Use a pair of small scissors, take your time, be careful.

You are finished. You have just completed your necklace and no one can tell where it begins or ends. Go look in the mirror. Enjoy! You have learned a great feat! Now you are ready to make a matching pair of earrings! This Channel type continuous crystal rope should go over you head 2 or 3 times depending on how you want to wear it. It can be made in many color combinations and several can be worn together for a great effect.

Loose diagram of ending knots between beads

Tighten-up diagram of knots between beads

PROJECT 3
EARRINGS

I'm not much of an earring person. I usually wear little antiques wires, gold or with a small stone that are insignificant. I usually wear a big necklace and that is enough. About four years ago my students all but demanded that I teach them how to make earrings. To this day, even though earrings are not as important a fashion statement, I still teach how to make earrings and you can decide on how simple or fancy you want them to be.

When I teach, I use what is available to me. So, when I measure, I substitute the length of my arm for the measurement of a yard. When holding the end of the fish line in my hand, I measure to the top of my shoulder, that is one length. Then I turn that length around and go back in the direction in which I have just come, holding both, this makes 2 equal lengths. When I have all the lengths I need for a particular project I cut at both ends.

Supplies

- 2 shepherd hooks or French ear wires
- 2 clam claw, bead tips that match the metal color of the wires
- 25 10 o round seed beads you can trust
- 2 larger beads, I like teardrops or bell flower shapes (8-10mm)
- 2 medium beads (6mm) faceted rounds
- 2 smaller beads (4mm) rondelles
- 2 "E" beads same color as seed beads
- 2 separate lengths or 2 one-yard lengths of 12lb. fish line

Step-by-Step Instructions

1 Make a double knot way at the end of one length so the beads won't slip off.

2 String on 2 seeds, then the medium bead.

3 Then string on 2 more seeds. (Here is where you can make it a shorter or longer earring by adding more seed beads).

4 Add the teardrop or flower bead, than the rondelle, then one "E" bead, then 3 small seed beads.

5 Now you are going to turn the entire thing around and string up the earring but **don't go through the last 3 seed beads** they hold everything else on. It is easier to string back through all beads if you ease them down by loosening the fish line as you go; string back through all beads. When you are back up to the top you'll probably have 2 very uneven ends so take both ends between the fingers of one hand and put the other hand on the bottom 3 seeds and pull. Now everything should be even. String the second earring the same way you did the first. When they are both strung and the fish line at the top is even, cut off the double knot at top of fish line that you made at the beginning.

6 Then pick up your first clam claw bead tip by its little one-sided hook. Holding it in this fashion you will see the tiny hole where the clam shell sides meet right in the middle. Put your 2 fish line ends through the hole coming in and up from the bottom, Now make three 1/2 knots, so they end up inside the clam, pulling tight, but not so tight as to freeze the earring between each knot. Make sure the knots cannot pull through the hole. When both earrings are done put a dot of Crazy Glue on the knot. Wait till it dries and cut the fish line very close to knot, this means pull it taut as you cut.

7 Using a flat plier or a long nose, (in this case, use the inner thicker part) close the clam. All your knots and cut ends will be hidden inside the closed clam.

8 Using the long nose pliers, put the claw or question mark part of the bead tip through the hole in the ear wire and pull around to close until it touches. **Don't smash shut**—the earring won't move.

You have now completed earrings of your own design to match your continuous crystal rope. Voila, an ensemble set!

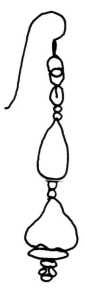

Full size earring— follow the beads as you string

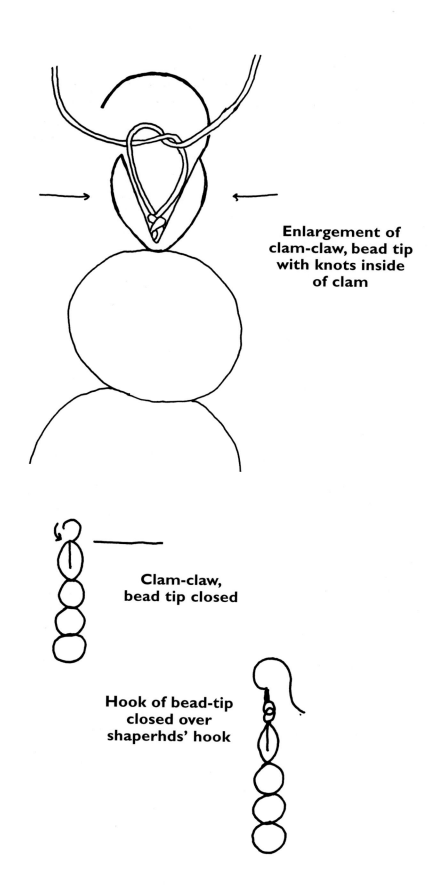

Enlargement of clam-claw, bead tip with knots inside of clam

Clam-claw, bead tip closed

Hook of bead-tip closed over shaperhds' hook

Buttons—Descriptions

Buttons can be a very innovative and original way to express yourself. Keep your eye peeled for interesting buttons. I love antique buttons; I buy them in all sizes. I use them as button-on endings, in necklaces and bracelets; I use them for interest or as charms. I use them to hold strands together on a necklace. There are several different kinds of backs on antique buttons, all are usable, but some are easier that others.

Shank buttons

Usually used for a glove or a shoe. Lots of black jet are available and inexpensive, 50 cents to $1 each. If you are a beginner, this is the best type for bracelets and button-on clasps.

Metal backs

If button has a beautiful front, you can use it as a focal point in a necklace and also hold your strands together, (use in the same way as a large bead, in multi-strands through big bead necklace). I call these "slide-through" backs. Usually they are on a larger button. They can be used the same way as a shank button. Often they were used as dress or coat buttons.

2-and 4-hole buttons

Buttons with holes are about the simplest buttons. They are found on shirts or blouses and even old underwear, often made of ivory, bone, horn or mother of pearl. If you were to use this type of button at the end of a bracelet you would merely string through it from back to front then front to back, putting some seed beads on the fish line in the front of the button to cover the fish line.

Glass or Molded buttons

Usually these were the more costly buttons. They come in all sizes but are molded out of one piece of glass. These are some of the prettiest but most breakable. The glass, as opposed to metal, will not yield, so if you force too many threads or strands you can easily break the button, Also when used in a bracelet, if you are not careful, they can crack or break, but they are worth it.

Metal buttons

Metal buttons are found on uniforms, they are the strongest because they are usually one piece. Brass buttons are one of my favorites but the ones I find the most irresistible are steel cut buttons. They are the most beautiful and also the most expensive, they usually have a shank back.

PROJECT 4
ANTIQUE BUTTON PIN WITH CRYSTAL DANGLES

Supplies

- 1 large button, old or new, with metal shank back, 1 1/2 inches in diameter

- 12 lb. fish line

- 10 o round seed beads (4 loops of a hank)

- "E" beads to match the seeds (75 count)

- Unusual colored "fancy" beads in various shapes and sizes to match color scheme

- 1 pin back, 1 to 1 1/2 long

- E-6000 glue

Step-by-Step Instructions

1   Using my method of measuring, cut 6 pieces of fish line each 1 yard long. Cut at both ends.

2   Using them altogether, thread through the shank of the button.

3   Now make a square knot using all the strands in the **middle** of the lengths. Thus 6 strands become 12 strands hanging from the back of the button. The strands will fall to one side of the metal shank just by gravity.

4   Taking each strand of fish line separately, pick up one strand. Start stringing seed beads up tight to the knot in the back of the button until you have cleared the bottom of the button. Then start adding your "fancy" beads using many seeds in between to separate the bigger beads. This way the flow of the dangles will remain fluid.

5   String until length of fish line is about 2 to 2-1/2 times the diameter of the button, if you desire it could be longer, but proportionally this is the best ratio.

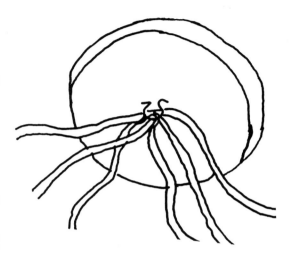

Back view of how to thread fishline through metal shank of button

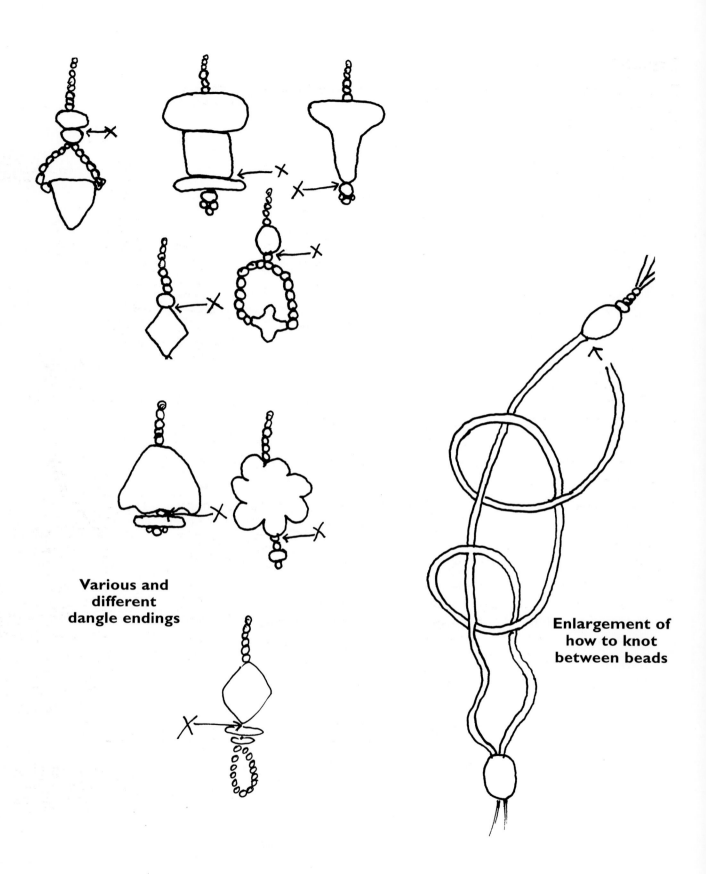

Various and different dangle endings

Enlargement of how to knot between beads

ENDINGS

There are a variety of endings you can use and I want you to practice all of them because it is the technique that you will be using as we go forward in this book to do complicated pieces of jewelry.

The X indicates the double knot, *you always want to knot **under** or **before** the bead you plan to hide your knots in.*

6 Following the fish line down, to the desired length, before putting on ending beads, (seed beads that you won't string through again) always put on 2 larger beads, one or both of these could be "E" beads. One of these bigger beads will hold the loop or bottom seed beads on, the next one will hide your knots. I call this the "set-up".

7 When you have done all this you are ready to knot and you should be going back up the strand you have just strung. When you are between the 2 bigger beads make your 2 slip knots by making a loop of the raw fish line that is held between your thumb and forefinger: Catch the end of the fish line (the tail) and pull it through the loop. Do it again. Then putting the second strand of fish line through all beads until it goes into at least a few seed beads. Pull second strand of fish line out of beads and cut flush. You need not glue. See diagram.

* (This is really much harder to describe in words than it is to do....soon it will be second nature to you.)

8 Repeat with each of the twelve strands varying the ending length slightly of each strand or dangle. As you finish each strand the bead ending will take on a symmetry of its own and you will quickly see how the last few should be made to compliment the others in length and shape.

9 Glue on pin back. If you are right- handed put the clasp on the left side and glue it on with E-6000 glue. This glue is preferable because it will fill any gap between the button and the pin back. Lay pin down flat on its face so pin can set level. Let it dry completely, overnight is best.

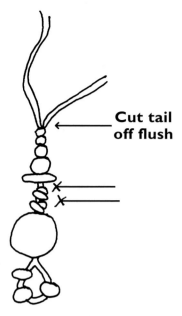

Cut tail off flush

Loose view of how to know between beads

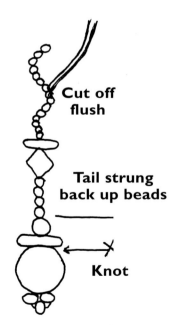

Cut off flush

Tail strung back up beads

Knot

Tighten-up view of how to knot between beads

ADVICE

Don't use more than 2-3 smaller (3-5 mm) beads in each strand. If you want to use some very large beads (6-10 mm) put them at the very bottom of the strand. *Less is more in terms of fluidity or movement and you want your dangles to move.* The knots do not necessarily have to be at the bottom but it is easier. If you must, you can double back up the strand and put your knots *under any large bead with a hole big enough to hide your knots inside.* There should be a pleasant little "snap" sound as the knots pop into the larger bead hole when things work just right.

VARIATIONS ON BUTTON PINS

You can make a button pin from almost any type of button or multiple buttons

WATERFALL BUTTON PIN

This can only be made with a button that has holes. Starting out in the very same way, tie strands in double knot in the back of button. Then reversing, pull fish line strands out the holes again so all strands are hanging in the front. With the holes vertical first bead the bottom strands putting bigger beads further down on the bottom because the top 6 strands will cover the top of the bottom 6 strands, falling over them. End the second or upper 6 strands shorter and more staggered, like a waterfall. (See colored pictures)

COMBINING BUTTONS

. . . in effect you are sewing you buttons together with the strands of fish line and making the dangles ready for stringing all at the same time . . . see diagram.

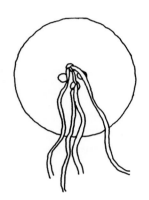

Strands coming back to the front of button for waterfall

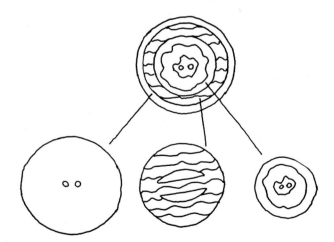

Front view of combining buttons

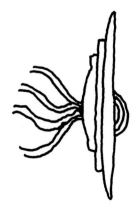

Side view of combining buttons

THOUGHTS ABOUT BUTTONS

I have some very strong thoughts about buttons that I would like to share with you. Antique buttons are miniature works of art and technology. They are also an endangered species. I feel by making them into jewelry I am making them immortal. Button collectors keep them on cardboard cards sometimes even framing them, but I bring them back into the light of day, so to speak, where they can again adorn, be seen, admired and appreciated.

Button collectors and dealers HATE people who make jewelry out of buttons because in 95% of the cases these people deface or mutilate the buttons by tearing off the backs or cutting off the shanks and then gluing them on findings or to each other. I do not do this. Actually I have become a button collector in a small way myself. I certainly have developed an appreciation and love for the beauty of buttons. In so doing, I have worked hard to find ways of using buttons so as not to destroy their original beauty or value. If you merely cut off the beaded dangles and remove the pin backs (E6000 glue very often can merely be pulled off if that is your intent) the button has not been harmed or damaged.

The same is true of buttons I use as centerpieces or closure in necklaces. Primarily, I use them as button closures. To use small buttons in a new and interesting way, without harming them please refer to the last project in my first book *The Bead and I* and make an antique button bracelet.

This ends the introductory section of this book. You have just graduated to the middle or the beginning of advanced beaded jewelry. You have just finished a simple necklace, a complicated necklace, a simple pair of earrings and a complicated pin. You have learned how to end a strand with no clasp, knot between beads, precision knot beads into place, make a beetle knot, do 1/2 of a 1/2 hitch, which I call "Marla's braid", use bead tips, finish the ends of dangles using several different designs, use Conso cord, use fish line, and use your first button without harming it. Pat yourself on the back, wear your newly created pieces of jewelry and soon you will be getting compliments from people noticing your attractive accessories and asking where you bought them. How does it feel to say, "I made it myself", when people ask? Let me know!

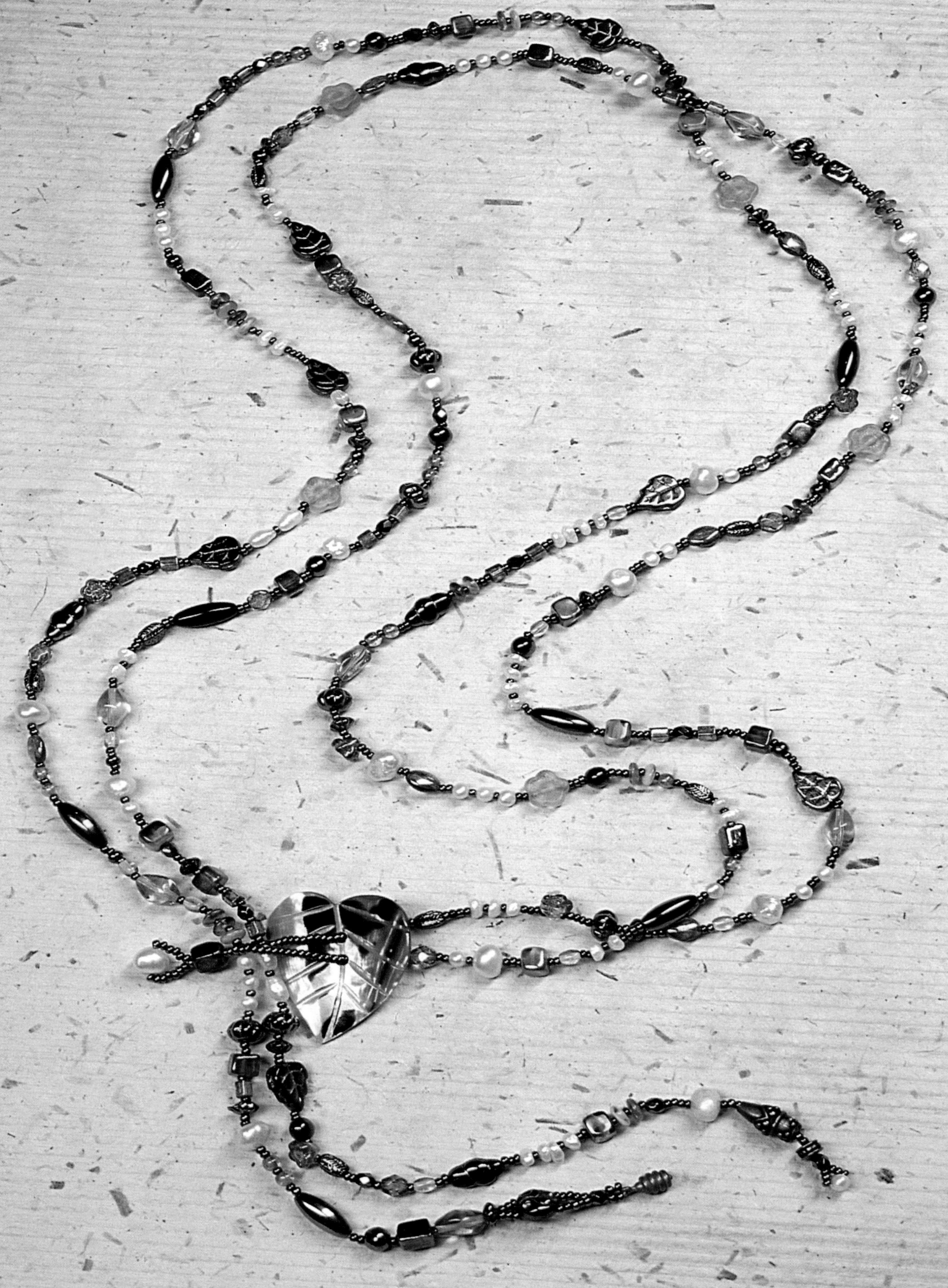

SECTION 2 ROUND-UP

PROJECT 5
TRICK LOCK DOUBLE LARIAT

Supplies

- 12 lb. fishline

- 1 medium to large button that matches your color scheme with 2 holes that are large enough to move seeds beads through.

- 6 loops or 1/2 hank of size 10 o seed beads

- Enough pearls, crystals and "fancy" beads to string two strands 46 inches long each.

- 2 stone or metal charms to match color scheme

- 16 mm "fancy" bead, small "pi" or unusual shape

Step-By-Step Instructions

1   Cut one length of fishline that measures 6 yards in length. Coming from the back or the wrong side of the button, thread naked fishline through it. From the right or front side of button string on 20 seed beads then string on a 6-8mm bead, a small "pi" or some shape that will hold the seed beads away from the button holes.

2   Pull the unit to the middle of the 6 yard length and then put 3 seed beads or 1 seed bead on to hold this larger bead or shape away from the holes in the button. Then string back in the direction of the button using 20 more seeds.

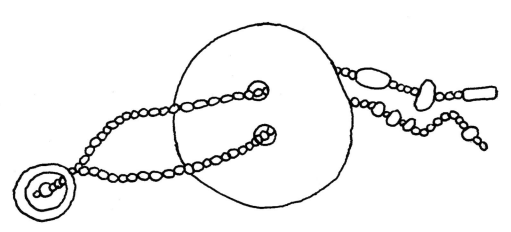

**Button facing drop
seed beads coming through holes
through ring, turn inside ring
and go back through buttons**

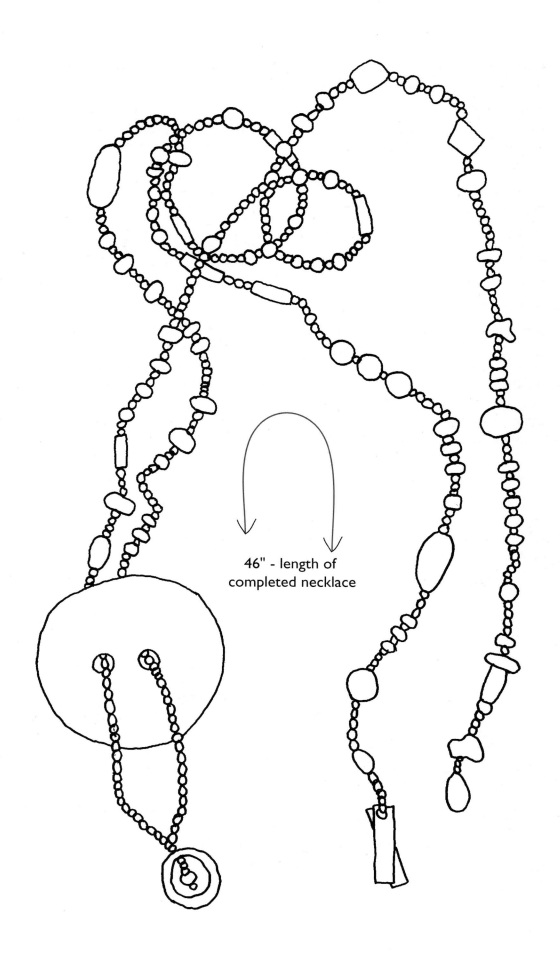

46" - length of
completed necklace

3 Now on the far or back side of the button, string on seed beads only for 2 1/2 inches on each strand.

4 Then continue to string each strand separately, away from button, using your pearls, crystals and "fancy" beads. Line up each strand, as you string, noticing how they will fit together and lie next to one another for the next 45 inches. Vary your colors and shapes.

5 When each strand measures 45 inches, end each strand individually with a charm or larger bead or bead story. To refresh your memory on ends refer to project #4, Button Pin. Pull tightly all the way back down the strand to tighten before knotting off between end beads as in a dangle. Vary length ends slightly by 1/4 to 1/2 inch. see the diagram of the full necklace.

Variations And How To Wear It

To wear wrap around your neck twice, making four strands, and then drop the two finished ends through the v-shape the seed beads make in front of the button. Drop the button down like a guillotine to secure and hold the two strands. Pull button clasp to the side of the neck so that it pulls against itself and holds tightly. This is a very impressive and dressy looking choker. Sedate and yet it has the romance a couple of well chosen charms can provide. Enjoy!

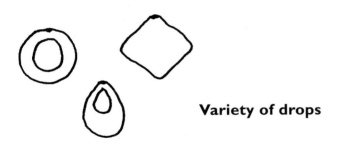

Variety of drops

Variety of buttons

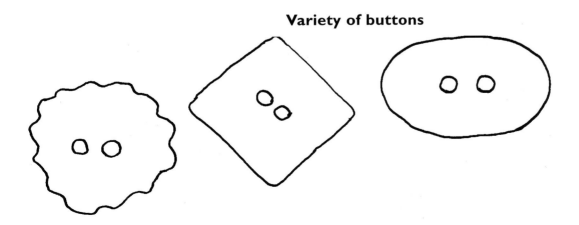

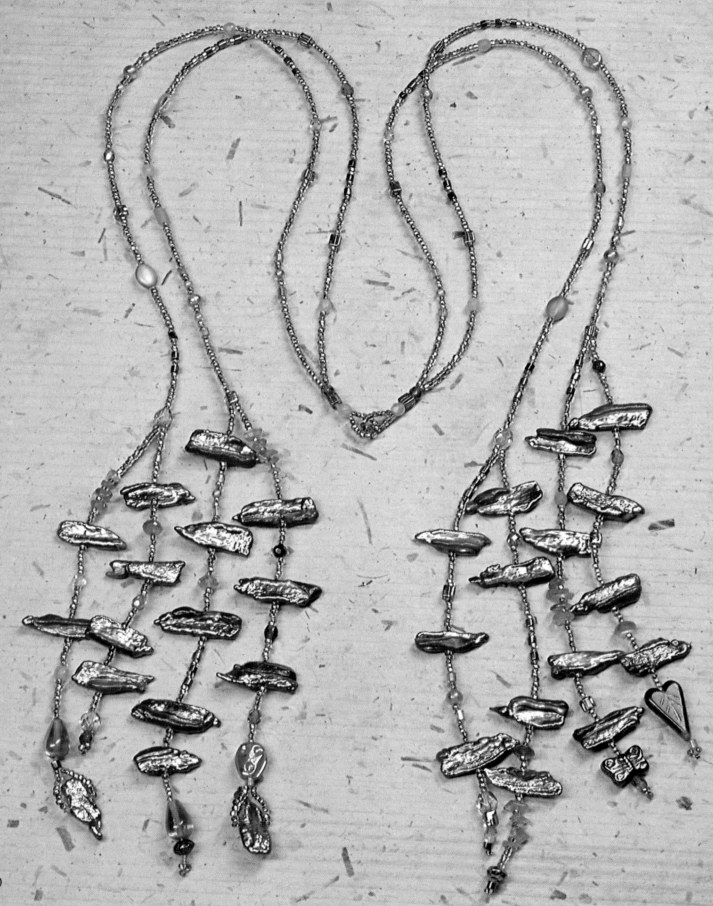

PROJECT 6
THE TREE BRANCH LARIAT

Supplies

- 12 lb. beading filament (fishline)
- 1 hank of 10 o or 11 o seed beads (must be able to get two strands of fishline through seed beads)
- 3-5 different kinds of small "fancy" beads and pearls, a strand of each, 5mm or smaller, and different shapes.
- 30 or one strand of "wing" pearls
- 1 strand (count 50) of 4mm faceted "magic" beads in color scheme
- 16 medium size 5 to 10mm for ends
- 50 "E" beads to match seeds

Step By Step Instructions

1 Cut 4 strands of fishline, 2 yards or 2 arm lengths long each.

2 With two strands together, string on 15 seed beads, turn and put all four ends through a small faceted 4mm "magic" bead. See diagram at right. (the term **magic** bead comes from the "The Great Rope Trick" project #9 of *The Bead and I*, I always refer to a 4mm faceted bead as **magic**). Now tie 2 naked fishline strands over the other 2 ends to make plain tie knot, and cover that by putting all 4 ends through an **E** bead or bead with a larger hole to cover the knot.

3 Bead down using two strands of fishline in the seed beads and adding small fancy beads to the length of 11 inches and then bead the other two fishline strands together to a length of 12 inches. End each with a larger bead.

4 Now split one side of the necklace into 4 separate strands (2 from each strung strand) and string separately with your "wing" pearls, 3-5 per strand with seed beads and larger "fancy" beads between them. Set up a bead story (a design made from several larger beads) to hide your knots in at the end of each strand as you usually make dangles. Make ends 5 and 1/2 inches long from split, finishing the ends within 1/4" of one another.

5 Do the other side of the necklace in exactly the same way. The total length of the necklace is 18" from the top intersecting loops.

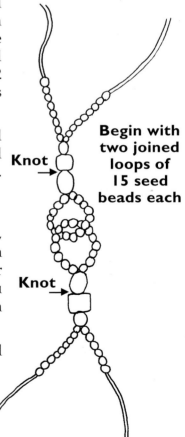

Knot →

Knot →

Begin with two joined loops of 15 seed beads each

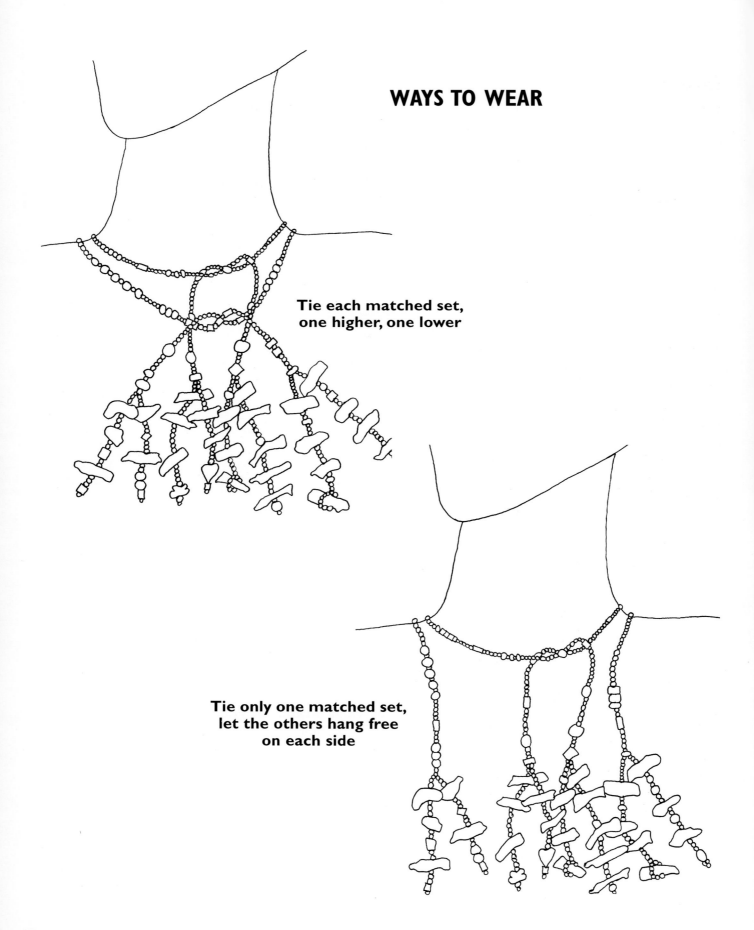

WAYS TO WEAR

**Tie each matched set,
one higher, one lower**

**Tie only one matched set,
let the others hang free
on each side**

VARIATIONS

The idea of this shortened lariat is to make it resemble a tree turned upside down; narrow around the neck getting fuller on the bottom. If you wish you can emphasize this by making 1/2 your ends all shorter and the other half all longer, then take the four ends that stop at 11 inches and make them about 1 1/2 inches shorter and leave the four ends that end at 12 inches longer and then when you tie it on, tie the four longer ends, two over two, and then the four shorted ends, two over two, a little higher up. It will make a very interesting and new look on your chest . . . like an inverted tree! You can also tie one set (two over two) and merely let the other set hang open, two on either side of you chest. See the diagrams on opposite page.

The other variation is to use larger seeds at the top, like 8 o and then switch at the split to 10 o seeds. I have lately become fascinated with charlottes, they are 13 o so you can only string through them once, but I have been doing this necklace with 10 o at the top and the same color charlottes at the bottom. Who says you could not even change color of your seed beads from the top to the bottom. I haven't tried this effect yet, but now that I am thinking of it, I want to try it. Maybe I'll try it in the colors of the trees that flower in the spring (pink and green)! If you want to make the entire necklace in charlottes, go back to project #9 in the first book and start it the same way with each strand 7 inches of seed beads across the back and make each side about 16 inches (stringing each strand separately) before doing the bead story ends.

A

B

C

PROJECTS 7, 8 & 9

"LITTLE JEWEL" LARIATS

INSPIRATION

These one strand, double length lariats were inspired by two things: first, the woman who represents my wholesale work is always encouraging me to find less expensive ways to express myself so she can sell my work at a lower price point. So, while I am most interested in making more complicated pieces of jewelry, I still try to keep an open mind and in this case, I took up the challenge.

In the process I decided I would also create an easier stringing pattern using simple repeats with the fancy beads and use the new Charlottes instead of my usual signature brown iris 10 o seed beads in-between. These tiny, 13 o one cut seed beads have begun to intrigue me because they have the look of metal chain in the colors of bronze, gold, hematite, and silver which make all the small 4mm beads, which I am so fond of, really stand out.

As the result of my experimentation I have developed a new stringing pattern and three variation on the theme of this one strand, double length lariat. In the following directions I give the variations between the three patterns all at once, so refer back to the big picture where they will be labeled A = with circular stone middle bead top, B = loop with larger bead top, C = long bead before dangle bottom (no special bead at the beginning, middle, dangles at the bottom).

Supplies

- 12 lb. fishline
- Assortment of 4mm or smaller, "fancy" beads, faceted beads, "E" beads or pearls to match your color scheme and seeds.
- Charlottes, 13 o in any metallic color I like the look of bronze
- Larger than 4 mm or combination of end beads to make a story or charm to make ends.
- Accent beads, in accordance with the variation that you are making:
  - one stone circle with a hole big enough to put a small be in the middle.
  - one larger, (8-10mm) round bead.
  - one large tube or long bead.

Step-By-Step Instructions (choose and study the variation picture before you begin)

I   Cut one length of beading filament (fishline) that measures 2 1/2 yards.

2   Beginning in the middle, this is where the variation of each type of lariat starts:

> **A-I** string on circular stone and fill the hole with a bead, if there is room put one seed bead on either side of the bigger bead within the hole.

> **B-2** string on your larger, round bead, add 1 1/2 inches or approximately 36 charlottes on each side of the bead and then string both ends into a small bead to close the loop

> **C-3** do nothing in the middle, merely start your stringing pattern both sides.

3   When you have done your middle, then establish your stringing pattern by choosing three or four different small beads that define your color scheme and repeat the order of them throughout the length of the lariat; separating each bead by the same prescribed number of Charlottes. Some examples of possible choices might be: 4mm faceted: "magic" beads, small pearls, stone beads or chips of stone, roundels, "E" beads. The count I used between my "fancy" beads was 12 seed beads between each and every one.

4   Continue stringing until both sides (measuring from the middle) measure 26" for variations A and B. Now is the time to start your "set-up" or bead story for your larger bead or charms. Some examples of endings might be: stone leaves or flowers, glass leaves or flowers, pieces of agate or cornelian or any proportionate size charm.

If you are doing C stop at 24"and string your tube bead onto both ends of fishline. If this bead has a bigger hole it may slide down the charlottes, this is fine because we will string another 1 and 1/2 inches of charlottes on the other side of the tube, so it moves, and then put a larger bead on both ends for a stop.

5   Finish the ends as you would in all other projects.

See the diagrams of the several ways these "little jewels" are worn.

Make note, in each diagram I have showed what is unique about that particular design.

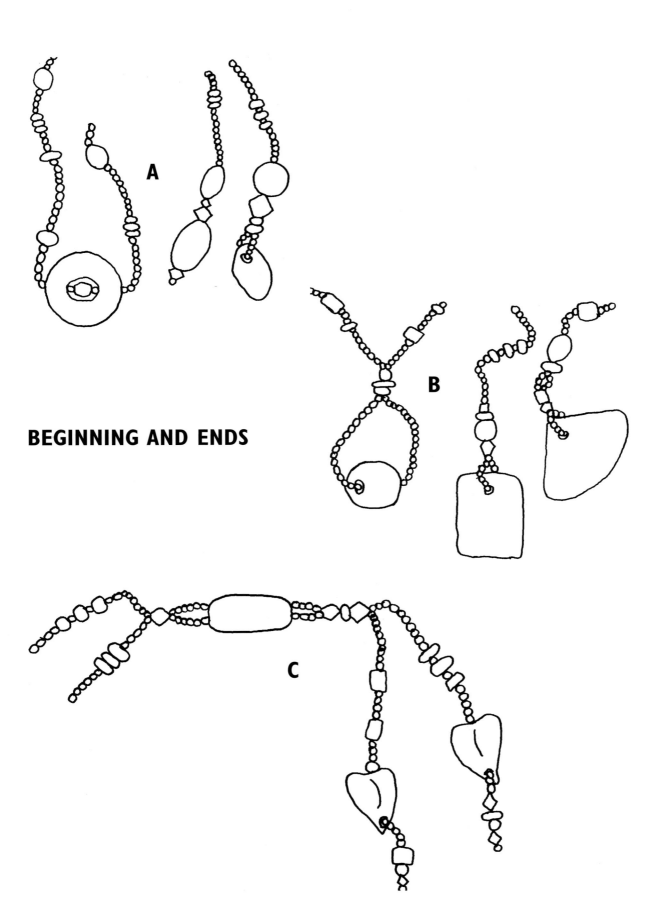

BEGINNING AND ENDS

A

B

C

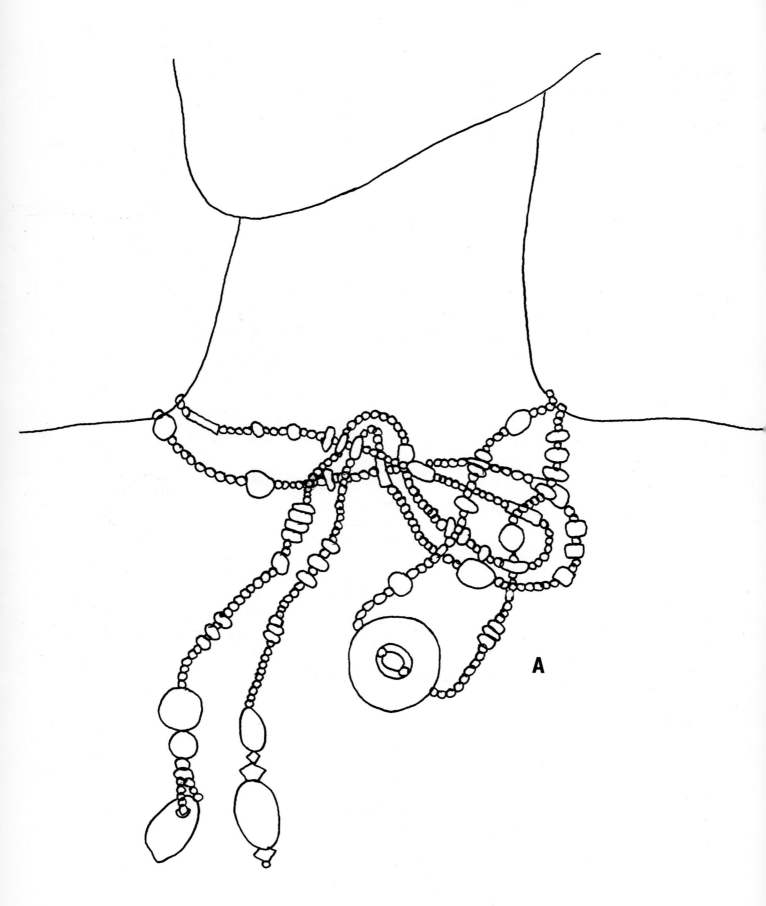

A

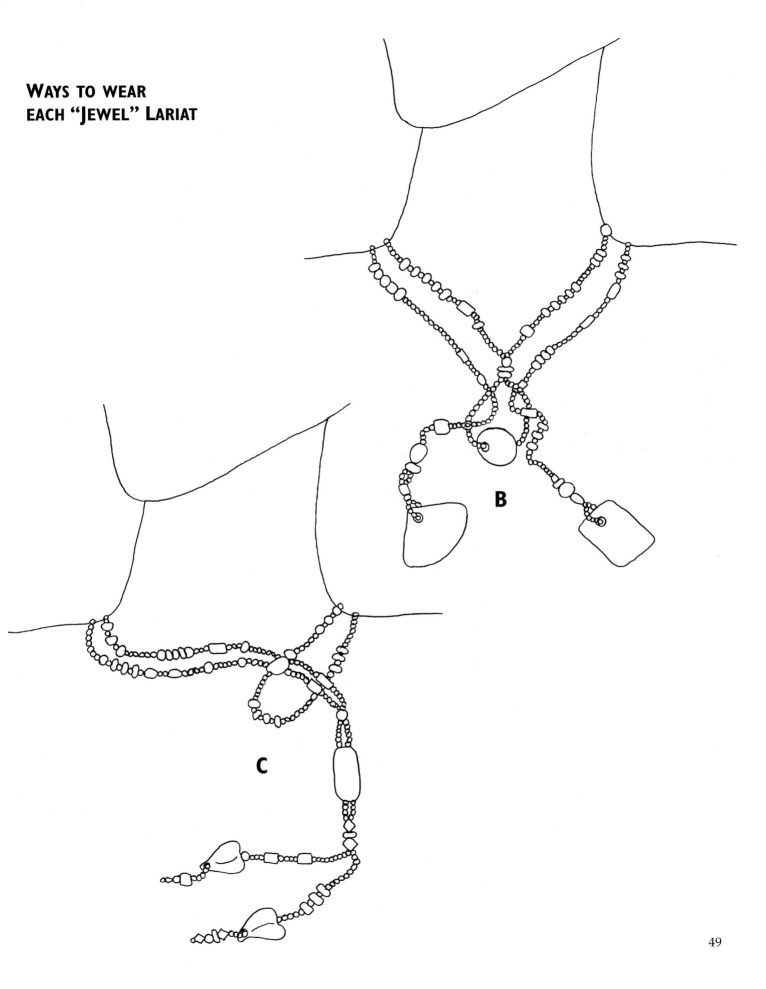

B

C

SECTION 3 STICKS, STONES AND DIVIDERS

Basically there are only three ways in which I create my beaded jewelry: using fishline, doing macrame' or using a needle and thread. In this chapter you will use all of them and most projects will include at least two of these techniques. The truly fascinating thing is just how much intricate jewelry can be created with just these three, simple techniques.

This chapter, in particular, is very exciting to me. Over the last few years I have found and worked with some very interesting new materials, as well as finding new uses for pieces I have been looking at for a long time. Now I am introducing them to you. STICKS, STONES AND DIVIDERS, is not just a cute name, even if it sounds that way; these are literally the very things you will be working with to create some astounding pieces of jewelry.

PROJECT 10
THE STICK NECKLACE

Of all the necklaces in this book, this is one of the few that requires advanced planning. You will be working with a thin, bone stick that has twenty-five small holes drilled vertically through it and every hole will have to be filled. You will have to search for about 18 to 25 small charms that will work well together in size and shape, a dozen medium and a dozen small beads to match your color scheme. Proportion means everything in this necklace, so searching out your charms and beads should be a process that you don't rush. It will take time to gather the proper components, but keep in mind that this is a collector's piece and one you will probably not want to part with once you have put it all together and worn it for the first time. Remember 25 of anything is a lot and that is what makes this piece such a knockout. The size of your charms should equal to a dime or smaller. One or two could be the size of a nickel, these will be the bigger middle pieces. Possible materials are jade (mine are jade), ivory, bone, serpentine, cornelian, silver, they could even be different handmade glass beads, if they are small enough, interesting and color coordinated.

My original stick was made out of ebony or bone and I found it in a shop that specializes in ethnic and imported beads and findings. When I bought it, I had no idea what I could possibly do with it. I just liked the look of it. It sat in the puddle in the middle of my studio floor for over a year where I saw it in my peripheral vision almost every day as I passed by. One day, suddenly, something clicked. For the next several days I pulled out every small jade charm I had been accumulating for eons and played with them until something pleased me. Then, I started experimenting with techniques. I dismissed fishline because in these very close space, it was too stiff and I decided to use a needle and thread. Though this necklace is not really sewing, I always celebrate the comfort of coming back to use of a needle....I am like a child, playing with familiar toys.

In the end, I fell in love with the concept of this necklace. It looks so astounding on that I knew I would have to reproduce it. I had to have more sticks. I also felt this would be a wonderful and special piece to share with my advanced students. I spent the next year discussing having the sticks made with several of my suppliers.

I guess the Universe wanted me, and you, to have the opportunity to create a new type of necklace. One of my suppliers was very tenacious and I now own over fifty sticks, and can have more made for me. You can buy a stick from me, cost: $20. Meanwhile, if you think you want to make this one of a kind necklace, read all the directions and then start collecting your special charms and beads. It is well worth the time and effort it takes to make this show-stopper necklace. It will be a beautiful addition to your collection of special things.

Supplies

- The stick

- Long English beading needle size 10 and your favorite choice of strong colored thread that will match your beads, I use Nymo.

- 18-25 small charms (only two as big as a nickel, all the rest a dime size or smaller) in your choice of material: jade, serpentine, cornelian, bone, wood, etc.

- seed beads no smaller that size 11 o if you can get through them more than once (it must be twice and preferably 3 times) 10 o is my preference.

- Conso size 18 in brown or black (I used brown).

- 15 medium (5mm to 8mm) interesting beads to match color scheme in stone or glass.

- 15 small beads (5mm and under) to match.

- Knotting board and T-pins.

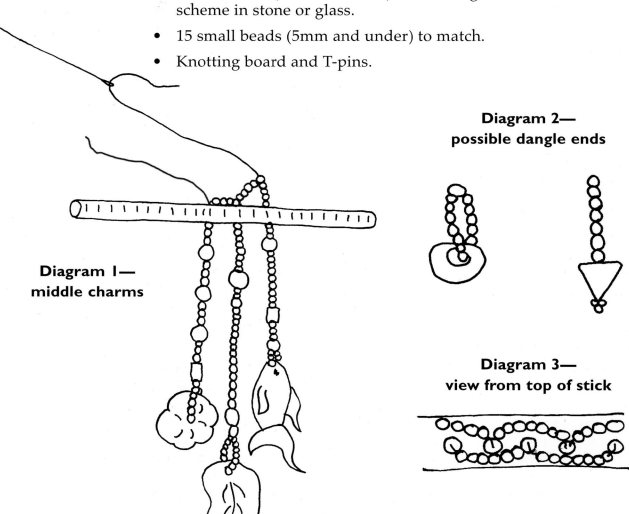

**Diagram 1—
middle charms**

**Diagram 2—
possible dangle ends**

**Diagram 3—
view from top of stick**

54

Step-By-Step Instructions

1 You will be doing this more than once during the course of creating this necklace: lay out your pieces, arranging them in varying lengths. As in the picture, if you are using a few bigger pieces, put them in or near the center.

2 Starting with a middle piece, thread your needle with the longest thread that you can comfortably handle and go down into the stick from above and into the middle hole. The longest charm or charms hangs down 3" from the stick and should go in or near the center. I suggest you place a bead or small bead story part of the way down, if it works with your design or charms. String down from the stick adding beads directly proceeding your charm, then your charm at about 2 1/2 or 2 3/4 inches, end either in a loop, or with a one bead or three bead bottom, diagram 2, and then go back up the length of seed beads, for a second time, through all the beads on that string and though the stick. This sounds difficult, it is not, it only needs some thought because the first charm sets up the pattern for all the rest. Diagram 1.

3 Now you are back at the top of the stick with the two ends of the thread coming out of the same hole. Pull the thread so you have an even amount on either side. This should be easy to do provided you have not split the thread . . . if you have, just use the ends at the length they are now. Put needle on one of the threads, it does not matter which one. Choose the direction you want to go, to the right or the left, it does not matter which way you go first. String on enough seed beads to get to the second hole in the direction you are going, usually 2-4 seed beads. You are skipping one hole, for now, covering it with beads. Diagram #3. Go into the second hole and arrange the charm you have decided goes there. I generally do all the longer dangles first. Then do the shorter ones in the in-between holes on your second pass. This fills in the top holes and spaces in-between. Vary the lengths according to how the charms fit together. Make it interesting.

4 Complete stringing your charms into place, every other hole, moving in that same direction and getting there with seed beads on the top of the stick until you run out of thread above the stick. Tighten and let any thread that is not long enough trail or leave out, we will finish the tails later. It is easier to get the charms to make the correct design, when you place them in every other hole first. Then in the very same way, doing your second row, put the middle sized charms in next, merely moving the seed beads covering the hole aside to get into the hole. (If your thread is short, you can also end it on the strand by knotting over the strands as you end any dangle and then hide the tail back up the seed beads and clip.)

5 Leaving the thread tails untied allows you to go back, if you must, to readjust any charm you are not pleased with. You can choose to fill the last hole on either end with a charm or leave it empty, I have done both. It depends if it crowds your design too much or not. When all the charms are placed, finish all tails by going back through top seed beads and knotting them off there. There might be as many as three rows of seed beads on top the stick. It is by stinging back and forth through these bead holes that you have been traveling when you fill the second tier or in-between holes.

6 When the design of charms pleases you and all remaining threads have been knotted off and hidden you can begin the sides from which your stick will hang. Using the simplest and most primitive method focuses all the proper attention on the charms and stick. Cut two separate lengths, one for each side, of Conso thread that measure 6 yards long each. Make two overhand knots, one over the other, half way down at 3 yards, (in the middle on each length) and then set the other length aside. Bend one length in half by merely holding the two ends, knot in the middle. Using the knot as an anchor, string a bead on both ends under the stick or do a bead story here if the hole is empty, and pass the two ends through the hole going up to the top of the stick. If the end hole has a charm strung in it, merely thread the ends leaving only knot, as an anchor, to through the stick with two threads of Conso coming out of the stick, going upwards.

7 When you are above the stick, you can either embellish here by adding one or more beads on both strands or merely start doing "Marla's braid". Go back to introductory project # 1 (Floating Fantasy) and review. Practice this braid on some yarn before you start on Conso so you will not ruin it. Pin Conso down to your knotting board with "T" pins and go very slowly so the braid is even and perfect. When you get a few inches from the end, tie an overhand knot with both strands, pull tight and embellish with a small bead as we did at the end of floating fantasy to trim. Tie it on and run to the mirror.

HOW EXCITING IS THIS SPECIAL NECKPIECE?   **ENJOY!**

"STONES"

Necklaces inspired by stones

These two necklaces were inspired by a woman named, Diane Karzan. She is in my bead guild and does beautiful work bezelling smooth stones and making them into necklaces. I was taken with the natural colors of the stones, their dull smoothness juxtaposed to the sparkling beads. It was several years later that I came across both the natural flat stones that had been drilled at a bead show and some larger beads that appear to have been acid washed to give them the look of river stones. I bought both of these and the next two necklaces are the results, so far, of what has prevailed in my creative research.

I worked with each bead and stone individually, embellishing it. The continuity of the entire piece was held together by repeating the same beads and colors to some extent on each bead or stone, though when you observe each one you will see no two look alike. It was only after beading all of the pieces that I then began to experiment with how I was going to combine them in a neckpiece.

Again, the key here is proportion. I really cannot emphasis this concept enough, because when the proportion of a piece is incorrect the eye cannot get beyond it. I know you have all had the experience of looking at something and squinting because something appears to be wrong. It is unnerving. Even if you cannot name it, the chances are that it is the proportion used in the piece that is wrong. There are no two places where this mistake jumps out at me more than the wrong size furniture in a room and in mismatched components put into jewelry. I cannot give you any hard and fast rules for getting you to the correct proportion because mostly I innately just feel and know it. In jewelry, I would be willing to say that it is about 1/3 embellishment to the size or the length of piece being embellished. I encourage you to experiment and play with it and also to try to train your esthetic eye to take notice when things appear to be either right or wrong. Like anything else it is a matter of awareness in combination with training your visual sense.

The first necklace to emerge from my stones study is this necklace, "Beaded, stonelike, Beads". I took the original one to the first show I was in after I completed it and it sold immediately. In fact, I tried to talk the woman out of buying it, to no avail. Then I had to track down more beads and start again. This is not always a bad thing because having sold it immediately makes me know that it works, thus giving me the impetus to continue researching my idea. Each time I do the same thing . . . all new again, I see it differently and invariably add something to the process, hopefully something better.

PROJECT 11
BEADED "STONE-LIKE" BEADS

Supplies

- 1 strand of 12mm or 14mm oval shaped, acid-washed beads in a soft light gray or beige color, that look like stones. This necklace uses 7 or 8 beads.

- 3 different color or types of seed beads 10 o, 11 o, 13 o. I used brown iris 10 o, pearl finish gray, 10 o, and antique French cut steel seeds. Pick any 3 that make your color scheme pop.

- 1 strand each of large pearls 6mm and small pearls 3mm in colors to match, mine were small, light gray and large, darker gray.

- Many small (under 5mm) and interesting shapes of beads. Look carefully at the picture and you will see, a few flat pearls, both long and round, roundels, faceted, "E" beads, small lapradorite chips, anything small and interesting....**remember proportion!**

- Unbreakable, matching thread of your choice to go through a long English beading needle, size 10. I use Nymo, size D.

- Lightweight tigertail or flexwire, if that is what you are used to using 1 yard or a long enough for the finished length necklace you desire.

- 4 crimp beads, and a clasp in silver or to match your metal color.

Step-By-Step Instructions

* in all following cases the word *stone* refers to a large stonelike bead

1 Taking each stone individually, thread your needle and anchor some seed beads to the front of the stone, by going though the holes. Then make another pass through the stone and start adding the more interesting beads by anchoring them through the seed beads, building into a form or design on the front of the stone. Take note of all the different shapes and forms I have used on mine. See picture.

2 It is hard to know when to stop. We are embellishing approximately 1/3 of each stone. We want to see the dull color of the stone look beneath, around or on either side of the embellishment. See diagram

3 When you are finished embellishing beads, start playing with them. I mean, arranging them to form a necklace. I often make more beads than I might finally use in any one neckpiece. The object here is to make them look as if they flow, visually, each bead into the next.

4 When you have the stones in a pleasing arrangement, decide what you want to put in-between them. I used one large pearl to keep the continuity. String through the natural holes of the big stones, using lightweight tigertail or flexwire. When you get all the embellished stones strung on with a big pearl between each embellished stone end with a big pearl at each outside end. Finish each side by stringing on all small pearls, or the same number of seed beads of your choice, between the small pearls in a repeat design. This is meant to be a relatively short necklace with all the embellished stones going from just behind one ear to behind the other ear. Put crimp beads on, (I use two in a row, on both ends) the clasp, and crimp to finish.

VARIATION

The brief necklace pictured in the middle of this one in the photograph came about while I was making the bigger one. On one bead in particular I got carried away with my embellishing and it did not look right with the all other beads on the bigger neckpiece, so I decided to make it into a small necklace of its own. My best friend could not stop commenting about it at dinner that night, so I took it off my neck and gave it to her. This is a perfect example of how new work evolves. I could have probably hung this bead vertically as well, with a small drop bead beneath it and then put simple beads up either side.

There is also the option to "over embellish" between beads, which would then be done after the necklace is completely strung. Now thread your needle and embellish the ends of some beads and on or around the large pearls in between. This would make the embellishments flow, but be careful not to over do which would defeat the purpose of seeing the "stone" effect of the underneath bead. Too much embellishment would make this look like one of those heavy, overdone neckpieces than never know when to end, with globs and gobs of beads and little emphasis on design or negative space.

The third piece pictured in the middle is a pin. The technique for making this is given in Project #12, Freeform, Found Object Pin, page 63.

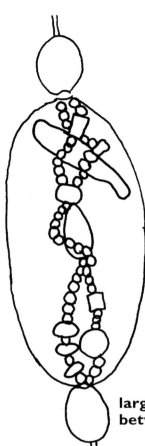

Stone like acid washed bead

larger pearl or beads
between embellished beads

PROJECT 12
FREE FORM FOUND OBJECT PIN
Use all the tiny treasures you love to collect

Supplies

- Ultra Suede in a neutral color (I like taupe or beige)
- Thin cardboard (as in shirt or back of paper pad)
- 10° beading needle, Nymo thread to match Ultra Suede
- Various beads in sizes 6mm and under to match or compliment your found objects. (Delicas and "E's, too)
- Oriental craft scissors or any scissors that cuts sharply right to the tips or points.
- Pin back 1 to 1 1/2 inches long (best quality you can find)
- Awl or sharp pointed instrument to make a small hole

Step-by-Step Directions

1 Arrange your found objects on the Ultra Suede until you are pleased with the arrangement of the larger pieces.

2 Using a Popsicle stick and small dabs of Barge cement fix your bigger objects in place on the Ultra Suede, (a 4 inch square of suede is big enough) Cut out 2 square shapes of the Ultra Suede. One for front and one for the back.

3 Link objects by sewing them down with chains of seed beads, or going in and out of the holes in objects, interspersing larger beads. I like to pack beads tightly in several areas and also leave some negative spaces. (see pictures)

Beading around found objects to create a shape for your pin

4 When all your beading is completed, draw a line with a pencil or a pen (if you cannot see the pencil) to create the free form outer shape you desire. It should be about 1/4 inch away from beads or found objects and then cut that shape precisely out of the suede with your sharp pointed scissors.

5 Now place the beaded shape on the cardboard and draw an outline on the cardboard of the shape. Then spread Barge Cement on the cardboard evenly and quickly right out to the line.

Draw line with pen or pencil, this is the cutting line

Place Ultra Suede piece down on the cement and press firmly down on all edges. Go back with a toothpick or Popsicle stick and get glue under any edge that is not firmly fixed. Barge Cement dries quite quickly! Cut cardboard out to the shape of Ultra Suede.

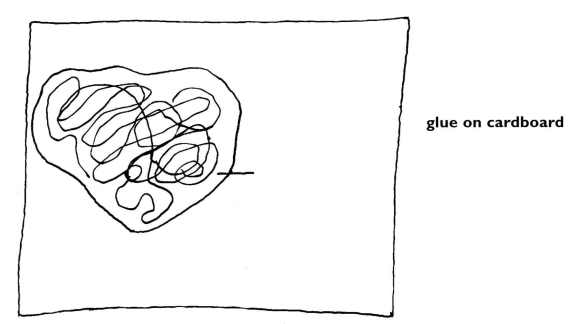

glue on cardboard

6 Then on the other piece of matching Ultra Suede, with the right side up, trace the outside shape with a pen (don't get too crazy if you use the wrong side here, there is very little difference in the look and no one will notice) Cut this piece out precisely.

7 Now turn pin face down with the back piece of Ultra Suede facing up. Place your pin back where you think you will want it (if you are right-handed, place closure side to the left). Pin back should be on the upper 1/3 of the pin for balance. With a pen, make a dot on the suede just below either side of the of the pin, (the joint and the closure).

8 Now with an awl or sharp instrument, poke a hole into the Ultra Suede 1/8th inch above your pen dot, then cut into the hole in two directions to make it bigger, like a star.

9 Put pin back through Ultra Suede back, forcing joints through the holes on either side, so that only the pin joint and pin closure show through.

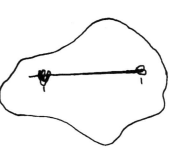

10 Cover the cardboard back with Barge Cement and apply the back Ultra Suede piece, with the pin through it, right onto the cardboard. Press pieces together at edges. With a tooth-pick glue all edges and let all glue dry.

Where to make pen dots to mark Ultra Suede for pin hardware

11 Now with your sharp scissors, trim all pieces together to match front and make a cleaner, sharper edge.

12 It is fun to sign your name and the date on the back with a thin felt tip pen. I give the pieces with the faces names which I also write on the back with the date.

VARIATIONS

This is my newest fun project for all the small things I cannot stop myself from picking up off the beaches like stones or shells, as well as all the wonderful mineral specimens that I collect. It gives me a chance to use all the small Delica beads, bugles and triangles that I buy in tubes. I have also incorporated the handmade ceramic faces from Fete'of Clay in Tucson and the handmade raku beads and "pi's" of Stan Roberts, who owns Xaz Beads, in Salt Lake City. I first worked with the Barge Cement in a workshop I took with Cynthia Rutldege several years ago and it opened a whole new range of possibilities for me. In fact, this glue was one of the most valuable things I have found recently, and it has expanded my designs, some of which are the projects in this book.

PROJECT 13
FLAT STONES

Supplies

- Flat stones
- Barge's cement
- Cardboard
- "Fancy" beads 5mm and under, interesting colors and stones
- Size 10 long needle
- Nymo thread
- Conso cord for sides
- Ultra Suede in neutral color
- Seed beads, "E" beads, pearls

Step-by-Step Instructions

After my initial experience with the acid washed beads, I was pretty well hooked on the look of stones. The great advantage of going to the bigger bead shows is finding new vendors and exotic supplies thus, I found the man who drills stones. In fact, I just saw him again at a show in Milwaukee and I told him about this book and my project with river stones and suggested listing his name so my readers could find him: his company is RIVERSTONE BEAD CO. Email: riverbeads@aol.com. His name is Anthony Shafton.

These stones have a completely different feeling from the beads because they are flat, but they are harder to work with and put to together. I started in the same way and chose five stones that related to one another in color and shape. I began to embellish. This time I used clear crystals, small round garnets, pearls and some antique red-tinted, steel-cut seed beads. The long oval stones were difficult to work with because everything had to be anchored to or through the one hole at the top.

My original thought was that I wanted to hang them on the ends of beaded strands, but there was no way to keep them from twisting around. Then I thought of embedding them in a neckpiece, but that was going to get too busy and would not have been the simple, more natural feeling I was after. They also were heavy and so they would require more support. This then becomes the very essence of how each technique builds onto the proceeding one, adding to our creative options as a designer.

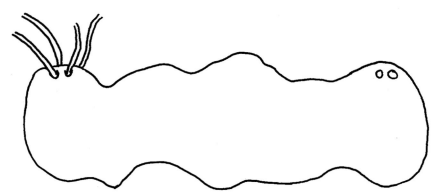

Diagram 1 — Make 2 holes on each side of final shape

Diagram 2 — threads coming down

Diagram 3 —

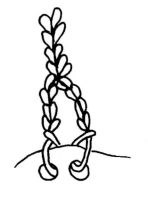

I arranged the finished stones in a pleasing manner and decided to utilize the more rectangle shape that they made together. Employing the technique I have outlined in "Free-form, Found Object Pins", I glued the back of the rocks to a piece of Ultra Suede and then went back to my needle and thread to embellish the surrounding and connecting areas, thus unifying my design. Next I supported the weight by gluing the Ultra Suede to a piece of cardboard and covering the back of the cardboard with a final piece of Ultra Suede. Then I designed and cut the outer shape of the entire finished piece. I contemplated making a large pin out of it, but decided I wanted a neckpiece. I put holes through all the layers and added my simple knotting technique from "Floating Fantasy" doing Marla's braid with one strand of Conso, going into each hole, knotted with two strands coming out, then meeting those two from the second hole to make four strands and then knotting these to the proper length to merely tie on. Remember you will need to cut your Conso to 4 times the entire finished length you desire.

Frankly, while this piece looks impressive tied on, I did not get the effect I initially had in envisioned. I think it will require some more experimentation using the new stone elements to achieve it. I have included it here mainly to intrigue you further with the use of stones in your work. A larger and far more impressive use of this technique can be seen in the inspirational gallery section pictured at the end of the book. In this piece I used handmade ceramic faces, pieces of natural colored matching purple shell and hand made raku beads. The names of the artist that make these is given in the "Freeform, Found Object pin" project.

Follow the Diagram numbers: **1** make holes through all layers of the pendant, two on each side, **2** practice Marla's braid, **3** do braid starting with two strands from each hole until long enough to join and then combine into a four strand braid. Finish with "fancy" beads on tail ends.

PROJECT 14
BEADED CAPS ON JADE RECTANGLES

Again I will take you on a small journey to illustrate just how easy it is to create, taking each technique you learn and applying it to make a unique piece of beaded jewelry. As I said before, I am apt to buy anything that excites me. It is only with my jewelry components that desire and lust alone can rule me. Over the years I have acquired many large rectangle and square pieces of jade that called to me mainly because of their natural patterns and coloration. While I am interested in making "big" necklaces, recently I have become interested in minimalism. This is a funny way to describe adornment, but think about it; often what we take away or omit becomes as strong a statement as what we might add.

My idea was to embellish merely this one beautiful jade rectangle and make it into a simple neckpiece. Thus reflecting the variations of colors naturally apparent in the jade which would step up my color palate, as well. Now I am painting a picture the top of this unique specimen with my beads. I have decided to call this bit of embellishment a beaded cap, but really I was only trying to emphasis the beauty inherent in the jade, itself.

These projects become the perfect place to practice a bead sport I have dubbed "dish-diving". Definition: searching in the little dishes of mixed beads that sit around my studio that never seem to get returned to their proper place, for just the "right" few beads that might be just perfect in my current project.

Supplies

- 1 flat large square or rectangle jade specimen piece that you love.
- 1 piece of Ultra Suede cut to a larger size than the upper 1/3 of the specimen, over the top, down 1/3 on back. Use jade piece itself to find proper size, see diagram.
- 1 hank 10 o or 11 o seed beads and "E" beads to compliment colors
- Gather many small beads (under 5mm) pearls, unusual shapes, Austrian crystals, 4mm faceted, in your color scheme or palette.
- 12 lb. fishline
- Barge's cement

Step-By-Step Instructions

1 To make your Ultra Suede shape, lay down your jade and draw an outline around it, starting 1/3 down from the top and then roll the jade over its top to the backside to 1/3 down from the back top. You can make it about 1/8th of an inch wider than the jade on the sides. Cut the shape out.

2 A perfect project for one of a kind beads or what I have dubbed "dish-diving". You are now in effect, working on an empty canvas, creating an original design with your beads. Judging from the shape of the piece decide on a focal point within your space (upper right, middle, lower left) could be some of your choices. Start with a larger bead, roundel, or found object. First attach it to your suede and then work around it building it bigger from the inside or closest to object to outside until it starts to fill the whole surface of the suede shape. You can also design a place where small proportional dangles might hang off the suede. Keep referring your beaded suede piece back to the jade so you can see where the beads are going to be on the jade. Carry your design over the top of the jade specimen and down the back a small part of the way. The backside of the piece should be flatter and less elaborate, so it will sit well on the chest. As you get closer to finishing, out toward the ends of the suede shape, make your beading simpler and flatter so it will fit closer down onto the jade.

3 At this point it becomes your choice and I have done it both ways, either trim the suede so that the side of the jade shows or else whipstitch the Ultra Suede so that it covers the sides and then embellish over the stitching. If you do the first one you will have to go back with a toothpick and glue suede down close to the edge.

4 Now that you have your bead cap shape made, it is time to apply it to the jade. Fit it over the jade. Cut two or more strands of fishline that are 2 yards long. These hanging fishline cords will later be beaded to make the side ties that keep this beauty on. If the jade is a bigger piece cut two or more strings. If it is smaller cut only two. The jade has a natural hole, but I have chosen to ignore it (beside you already covered it with beads). I do not like the way in which the jade would hang from the drilled hole. Place the middle of your fishline lengths along the top of the specimen and apply glue carefully under where your beading will go and glue beading down. Trim excess and continue to embellish any area that is not covered, by keeping your knots hidden in the beading.

5 When the glue is dry. start adding beads up the fishline sides with seeds and intermittent "fancy" small beads. I usually do a repeat pattern here to keep it simple. Finish ends as you would any dangles and tie it on. You could put on a clasp with beadtips if you want this to be shorter, but my design is of a longer necklace that can tie on at various lengths.

VARIATIONS

This same embellishment could be done on any large shape or object. One of my private students did it on a large crystal drop. The Ultra Suede is very easy to manipulate and can be trimmed to any shape. You might also suspend this piece in a more elaborate way with more fishline strands, using pearls or put conso under the cemented top and then do Marla's braid for a simpler look.

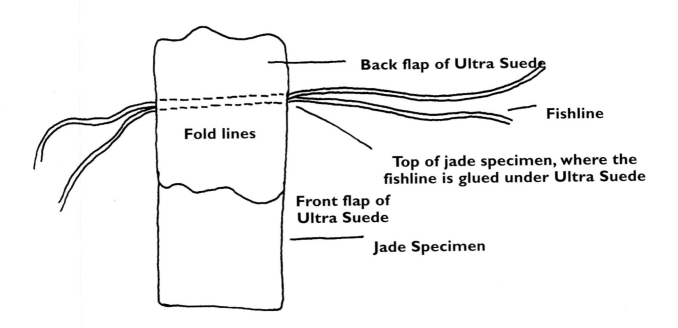

Back flap of Ultra Suede

Fishline

Fold lines

Top of jade specimen, where the fishline is glued under Ultra Suede

Front flap of Ultra Suede

Jade Specimen

PRUJECT 15
BONE DIVIDER CROSSOVER NECKLACE

Supplies

- 1 bone divider with 6, 7,or 8 holes though the width (side to side)

- 12 lb. beading filament (fishline)

- 1 hank of 10 o seed beads in a color to match your color scheme or brown iris.

- 12 bone charms or large bead combinations to finish ends, these could be buttons, shells, rings, small abalone birds or anything small and interesting.

- Combination of "E" beads and fancy beads under 6mm to match colors

- 6 long bone tube or hairpipe beads holes big enough for 6 strands

- 1 strand of 4mm faceted "magic" beads to match your colors

- 1 set of bead tips and clasp to match in silver or gold metal (your choice).

Find a place to work this necklace where it will not be moved until you are finished stringing it. Leave it taped down until you are finished working the bottom and lower sides. The masking tape will make marks on your bone if left on for more than 48 hours so plan a time when you can devote yourself to this necklace or remove tape in-between. You can remove stickies from tape with lighter fluid.

Step-By-Step Instructions

1. 12 stands of fishline that measure 2 yards or 2 arm lengths long, each.

2. Divide into two groups of 6 strands each and put each group of 6 ends through a nice bone hairpipe bead and then a "magic" bead (4mm, faceted bead) which will hold the 6 strands tight enough not to move. These represent the two sides of the necklace. See Diagram 1.

3. String one side of the necklace down from the bone bead for 5 inches, making each of the six strands a little different with your seeds beads and small, fancy beads and then merely eye ball and copy the same designs on the other six to make the other side of the necklace.

Diagram I

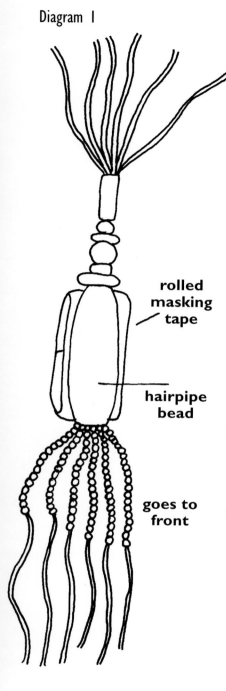

rolled
masking
tape

hairpipe
bead

goes to
front

4 Now push all the beads on all six strands one half way down the fishline so that there is 15 inches of empty fishline extending beyond the "magic" bead that is empty, this will become the back of the necklace and the remaining fishline, extending empty from the other end will be the front, about 24 inches. We will do the back of the necklace last.

5 Now roll up a piece of masking tape so it sticks on both sides and put it under the wrong side of the bone divider so that it sticks to the table and won't move. If it will make it easier for you, you can also put making tape under each tube bead to secure the sides in place, about 6" to each side of the middle. Measure the same distance from top strand, out to each side, then secure, keeping the divider in the middle.

6 Spread out your six strands, so the designs of each strand match on either side of the bone divider. Starting with the top two strands, one from each side, string through the divider, using a little larger bead before the divider hole on each side.. These beads can either all match or each pair can be different. String each succeeding pair of strands moving down the holes of the divider. Each will have to have some beads added to be a little bit longer to reach the next divider holes. Refer to the middle of Diagram 2.

7 After each pair of strands cross directions through the holes in the divider, also string through the first larger bead on the opposing side, leaving the exposed fishline falling down on each side. String all six pairs in the very same way.

8 Starting with the bottom pair stringing as you did down the side with seeds and small, fancy beads until this strand measures 5 inches from the bottom of the divider and then make your ending with big bead story or charm. Do the other bottom strand the same length. Moving back up the divider holes finish each pair of strands a bit shorter until they fill in, thus tightening the side strands as you end each one. If there are gaps, more sets of holes than six or if you want more dangles merely add an additional length of fishline through the divider hole and first beads, tightening them when the dangles on both sides are finished.

76

Diagram 2

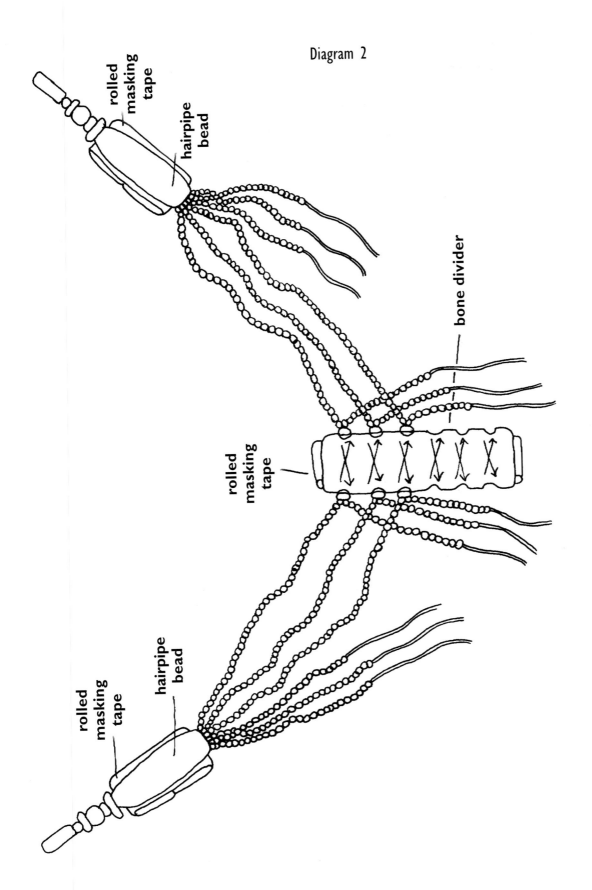

rolled masking tape

hairpipe bead

bone divider

rolled masking tape

rolled masking tape

hairpipe bead

77

Diagram 3

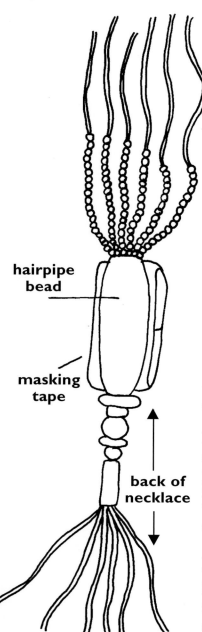

hairpipe bead

masking tape

back of necklace

9 Now to make the back of the necklace use Diagram 3, follow it in the opposite direction from the side haripipe bead. String the remaining 6 strands on both sides with beads that have holes big enough to get all 6 strands through them to the desired length you wish the necklace to be around your neck. Put all 6 strands into the clam shell bead tip end, divide ends in half (3 and 3) and make a square knot (two ties) pulling the knot tight into the bead tip. Put crazy glue on the knot and when dry cut off the remainder of fishline as close as possible (tug on the ends as you cut them) then close your clam over the knots and attach to the clasp of your choice.

Put on your necklace and run to the mirror and look at your creation. Add extra strands through bone divider holes if you want to make the bottom look fuller. This necklace was inspired by a trip to the Field Museum and observing American Indian jewelry. The dividers I saw were used in chokers, but I do not like to make chokers, so I reinterpreted the idea of using the divider, but added the crossover element and the dangling treasure charms.

I wish I could tell you where to find these bone dividers, but I can not find a source. You might look in all the ethnic booths or suppliers. Finding the bone divider will be a challenge, if you find a good source let me know.

VARIATIONS

Possible variations in making this necklace might be adding turquoise or canelian charms and beads with the bone. I think it is also possible to rub in some darker colored stain into the divider to make it a different or darker color. I look for these dividers at bead shows. They are definitely more primitive and ethnic so search for them in these types of booths.

Also some Deco jewelry, bracelets in particular, have pieces that might work in this same way. This necklace is designed to accommodate 6 holes, but many dividers have as many as 8 holes. In the case of 7 leave the middle one unstrung. In case of 8, skip hole numbers 3 and 6. Add additional fishline and charms through these empty holes after the necklace is finished The extra strands are secured when the opposite or second side is tightened, then neither side can move. This is the same principle as the tutti-frutti on the "Tutti-frutti, Carmen Miranda" Bracelet, in my first book.

SHOPPING

Beyond the Bead and I is the second manual I have written about designing jewelry with beads. This is also the more esoteric of the two books. Because I am always pushing what I already know to the furthest limits of my creativity, these pieces are even more unique than those in the first book.

My reputation as a designer is based on my ability to create one-of-a-kind pieces. Therefore, shopping becomes one of the most important and integral parts of the process. I once had a student from the Great Lakes Beadworkers' Guild, in Michigan, confess to me that on several occasions when I did a semi-annual bead show there, she would follow me around the room as I shopped the show. She said that she learned a great deal by watching what I chose to buy. At these shows I was a vendor, but part of my show experience is to get to see what things are on the other tables. I would ask a former student to work my booth for me for one hour, in trade for free beads, so I could shop the show.

I think of myself as a woman who was born to shop. Shopping is to women what doing sports is to men; it requires equal endurance. Being basically a gregarious animal, shopping for my beads is the perfect counterbalance to the large amounts of time I spend alone creating.

I want to share with you some of my tips about shopping that will help you to design your own one-of-a-kind jewelry, thus establishing your own individual style. The only thing that makes my jewelry different from any of my students work is the unique things I find and how I use them. I have told you the last part of this via the pages in this book and those in my first one, The Bead and I. Now let me tell you how to shop.

First of all, if you are trying to match something, take it with you to the bead show. I keep a small see through, zip lock plastic bag near my desk and this is where I put samples of things I want to match or find more. If you collect samples all the time, then you can merely grab this bag when you are on your way out to shop.

Always be at a bead show when it opens, if at all possible. The most unusual things get sold immediately and that is what I am after. Don't work the whole room or see the whole show before buying what interests you, buy it the moment you see it because it will be gone by the time you get back. Start to shop the room from the opposite side or direction of the biggest flow of traffic. This way you get to see the back end first while everyone else is bulked up at the opposite end and moving slowly. Look at each vendor's booth carefully even if you think you are not interested in the type of beads he is displaying. For instance, I do not make typical ethnic jewelry, but I have found some very interesting pieces in ethnic booths. Take a chance on buying an unusual piece that interests you even if you don't immediately know what you will do with it . . . you will never figure out how to use it if you don't own it and therefore are able to play with it.

In this book, the Stick Necklace was inspired by a funny stick drilled with twenty-five holes that I picked up in an ethnic bead shop more than two years ago. I had absolutely no idea what I would do with it, yet I was drawn to it and had to have it. It laid on the floor in my bead puddle for a year, until one day I picked it up and made an amazing necklace with it. So, buy that odd thing that fascinates you. Seeing it on a daily basis in your peripheral vision will register in the unconscious part of your creative mind.

If you are not sure what to specifically create, than pick a color you like to wear or work in, or pick a color you have never worked in and start buying beads in different sizes, shapes and finishes in or around that color. Let's say it is purple; well, buy some pink purples and some blue purples so you can move either way through the color. The variation in your sizes of beads or pieces may also suggest what might become a design possibility.

If you have read my first book and this book, then there should be certain things that will trigger your buying patterns. For example, if the disc necklace, is something that is of interest to you, than be on the lookout for three matching discs made from ceramic, glass, sliced geodes, etc. There are many focal pieces in the designs I have outlined in these two books. I am constantly on the lookout for unique pieces or the ones I need for certain designs and I keep them in my head while I am shopping.

When I see several or many of the same things in a booth, I never buy more than three of them and usually only two. A fellow artist once confided to me that when she sees something she likes that she buys all of it so no one else will get any of it. I generally take an opposite approach, which is that I don't like to buy all of something, believing it is better karma to leave something for others to share. Besides, I make one of a kind jewelry, so unless I am looking for a number of the same things because I am teaching a class, why would I need more than three. I get bored easily, so I never intentionally repeat a piece. Even when I have three of the same thing, it is only because I want to use it differently each time. When I am commissioned to repeat a piece, I only promise a customer that it will be "like" the original in feeling and then I purposely do not refresh my memory, or if so only by a slide or picture of the original in the hopes of creating it again in a whole new way; thus, a one of a kind.

Travel light, emptying your purse of all unneeded and heavy parapher-nalia and then put your essentials into a bigger carryall or backpack. Take your samples and check your checkbook before leaving home to make sure you have enough checks or cash if that is your preference. Wear comfortable shoes and take an extra pair with you, even if your feet hurt, they will feel better if you change to different shoes. Dress in layers of light clothing that you can carry instead of wearing when the lights make you too warm. Take a large bag or a small suitcase on wheels with a handle....beads get really heavy and the car is usually parked too far for frequent trips to unload things.

When I get home I am generally exhausted, but the first thing I do, after I catch my breath, is to go over my purchases and make sure I have all my receipts and cards in a safe place. One of the things I am not so good at is jotting down why I wanted this card on the back of it the moment it is handed to me at a show. Often by the time I get home, I cannot remember why I took that card in the first place and then the purpose is defeated because the name or logo means nothing to me. If you have a pen on a string or ribbon, it is smart to attach it to your body, neck or belt loop, so you are not always looking for it or someone else doesn't keeps it.

When you have more time, add your newest purchases to you cache or "puddle". I will not repeat myself here, but if you have not read about my habit of puddling, described at length, in my first book go do so right now...it will change the way you create with beads. I have also written about color and proportion in that book and I urge you to borrow it to read if you do not own the book yourself.

Included at the end of this book is a gallery of inspirational, one of a kind pieces which are variations of those described with full instructions in this book. They are meant to stretch your imagination. Remember creating is always asking the question: WHAT IF? What if I do it backwards, upside down, sideways? What if I use one, two, three, many? What if I changed the colors, mixed the colors, reversed the colors? What is the best use of each unique material? What if I made it short, long, single strand, multi-strand? What if I mixed unlike materials? Etc. I discuss this very provocative question at length and with visuals in my lecture, "How to Design One of a Kind Beaded Jewelry". If I am lecturing in your area, try not to miss seeing it as viewing the subtle differentiations is very provocative, in this instance, pictures are better than words.

I think shopping is one of the most exciting parts of creating, a kind of competitive sport. Remember that choosing unique and individual pieces is the beginning process of creating because these things spark your creative energy. Doing one of a kind pieces will make you stretch yourself and soon you will find your own voice and the direction you wish to explore further in your work.

SECTION 4 TASSELS

PROJECT 16
ANY BEAD INTO A BEADED TASSEL NECKLACE

Supplies

- 12 lb. fishline

- 1 large unusual bead (this is the perfect way to use a handmade bead)

- 2 hanks of round 10 o seed beads that go with your color scheme

- "E" beads to match seed beads

- 1 spool of nymo thread that goes through a #10 beading needle closest to the color of the seed beads.

- Many "fancy" smaller beads (6mm and under) and unusual shapes to make the bead ends of the tassel.

Step-By-Step Instructions

1 Determine the length you would like the beaded ends. My rule for proportion is approximately 2 and 1/2 times the length of the large bead. Make lengths no less than 1 yd. long.

2 Cut 12-18 lengths or any number divisible by 4, remembering that each length will bend over to become 2 beaded ends. Choose one length that is easy for you to measure, like the length of your arm and measure all lengths at the same time.

3 Then thread your beading needle and string on 15 seed beads and move them to the middle of the length. Thread next length of thread on needle and string through the same seed beads. Repeat this until there are 4 empty threads extending from both sides of the 15 seeds. See Diagram 1.

   Make an overhand knot of all empty ends as close as possible to the ends on loop shape. See Diagram 2.

4 Make a threader by stringing a long piece of fishline through a big eye needle or a doll threading needle and pull 2 long ends of threader through the big bead, leaving loop out the opposite end. Then put all unbeaded nymo ends through the loop and pull through large bead. The seed bead middles should now be bent over above the top of the large bead in a loop. If they slip inside the hole of the big bead you can either put a smaller (8, 10, 12mm) bead above it or else add an additional set of 4 lengths doubled over to make another loop at the top. (this is the most tedious and least creative part of the tassel—the setup)

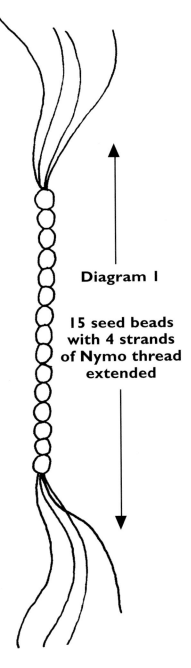

Diagram 1

15 seed beads with 4 strands of Nymo thread extended

5 Now threading one of your nymo ends separately string on seed beads until you get down to close to the final desired length and then do a "bead story" or dangle end (3 or 4 beads that make a particular shaped end) and finish as a dangle end, knotting between beads and the string ends back up the strand. Cut excess thread flush where it comes out of seed beads. (the first several strands of seed beads will fill up the large bead.)

6 Continue to design all ends of tassel, changing design and length about every 6 or 8 ends. This will give semitry to the finished tassel. Beginning with the longest length and design will make it easier to control shape but you can always go back and add more longer strands as you create.

When tassel is finished you can use it as a decoration on an accessory or piece of furniture or you can make it the focal point of a necklace.

7 To make a necklace merely string 2 or 4 pieces of beading filament (fishline) that measure 2 yards or lengths each through the loops extending from the top of the bead and string them separately as we usually do matching the sides in patterns of seeds, "E" and "fancy" beads.

8 Finish with traditional beadtip ends and clasp or larger bead and counterweight dangles as we have done in previous projects in the book *The Bead and I*.

**Diagram 2
knot inside
bead**

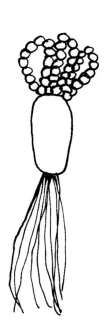

PROJECT 17
BUTTON IN THE MIDDLE OF THE TASSEL NECKLACE

Supplies

- 12 lb. fishline
- 1 hank of size 10 o seed beads
- Enough "fancy" beads to string on 8 strands that are 14 inches long each (tubes, crystals, round small pearls, "E" beads)
- 23 wing shaped pearls or any other unusual beads you wish to show in tassel.
- 1 medium to large button with 4 holes (abalone is the kind used in picture)
- 12 glass rings with a 1/4th inch diameter opening

Step-By-Step Instructions

1 Measure 4 lengths of fishline that are each 2 and 1/2 yards long.

2 Starting at the bottom of each of the 4 ends make tassel by stringing on pearls and fancy beads randomly, to make dangles, measuring for 4 and 1/2 inches. When all 4 ends have been made string them through button, 2 ends front to back, 2 ends back to front.

3 Taking 1 end from the back and 1 end from the front to each side (2 strands) string randomly as we usually do until each side measures 14" **exactly—measure each strand separately.**

This drawing shows the beginning, repeat this procedure for the ending, for a total of 8 dangles coming out of the button.

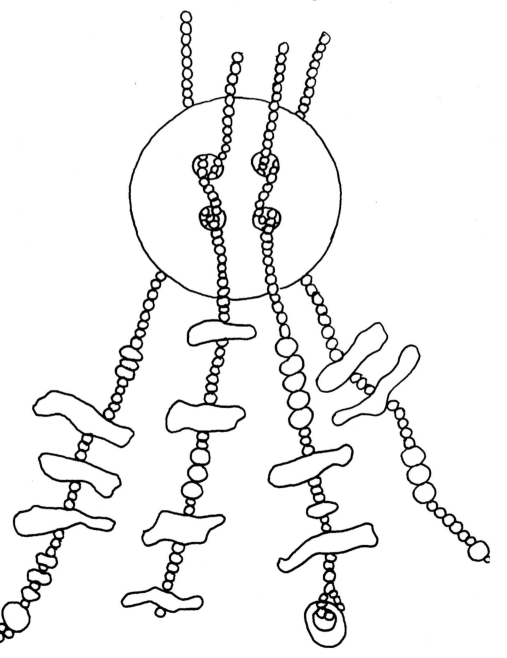

4 Then string a glass ring onto both sides, 2 strands coming into the ring from each direction and continue to string at random back down toward the button. **Make sure all strands measure the same length as the first ones—14″ from back ring.**

Diagram 2—I go in from each side to cross in ring

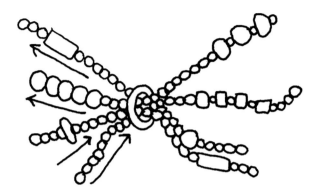

5 String through the holes in the button, 2 back to front and 2 front to back, and then finish these ends as part of the tassel with the winged pearls or the special beads that match your first ones. End in varying lengths, as in all dangles. Make your knots in larger fancy beads and go back up each strand through the seeds.

6 Divide each side the way they go through the glass ring at the back of the necklace and put your new necklace over your head. The button should be in the middle of the tassel. The front of the necklace is the front side of the button.

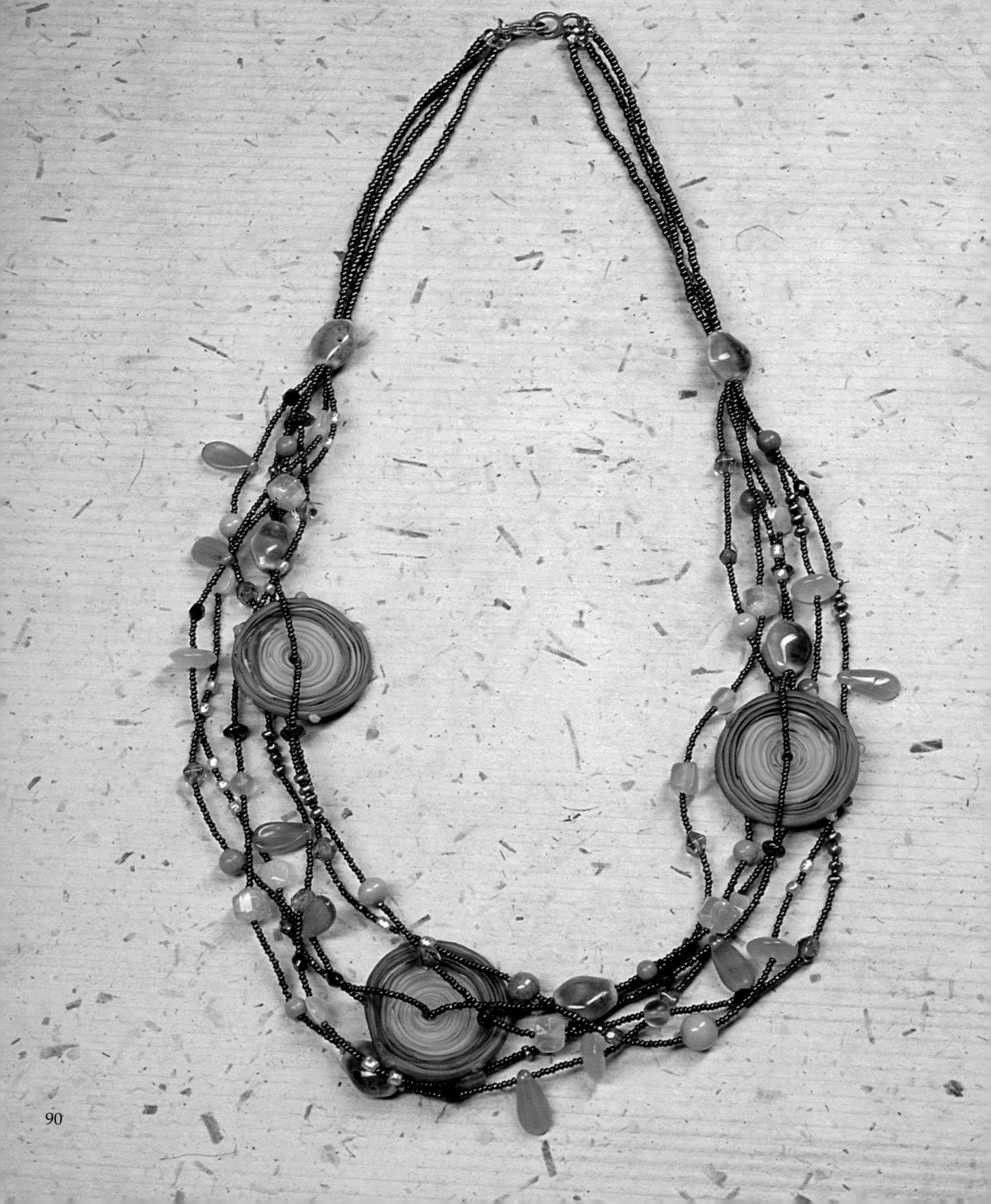

SECTION 5 DISC AND PIECES

PROJECT 18
THE DISC NECKLACE

SECTION 5

Supplies

- 3 discs 1 1/2 to 2 inches in diameter, alike or very similiar
- 12 lb. fishline
- 1 clasp for six strands
- 1 hank of 10 o seed beads and matching "E"s
- Enough "fancy" beads in varying sizes (4-6mm) , a few 8mm, also unusual shapes, small rondells, tubes, bicones, pearls, dangle beads to match your color scheme and string six strands on each side.

Step-By-Step Instructions

Find a large, flat surface to work where this necklace can be laid out as you work and won't have to be moved until you are finished. This is a necklace that was inspired by the disc or small "pi" pieces that fascinated me. If you like it be on the look out for 3 matching or like disc shapes to use together. I have also used ceramic discs, coins, mineral slices and handmade glass (the ones pictured here are made by Karen Ovington). They are very delicate and expensive, but they make a wonderful noise.

1 Puddle your supply of beads, choosing color combinations that heighten the beauty of your discs. Look at the cream pearls I have added and how they spark the green and brown of the discs.

2 Lay out the 3 discs across your work space.

3 Starting in the middle with the largest or most unusual disc, cut 6 lengths of fishline that are 2 yards long each, put 4 of them around your neck for the next two discs. String on enough seed beads to go around the disc, coming through the middle hole on one side and then link the two ends with a bigger bead when you are a little away from the disc. You can do a simple end over end knot here that is hidden in the next big bead to keep strands from slipping. Do the same with the other strand, on the other side of the disc, varying the distance and design of the beads.

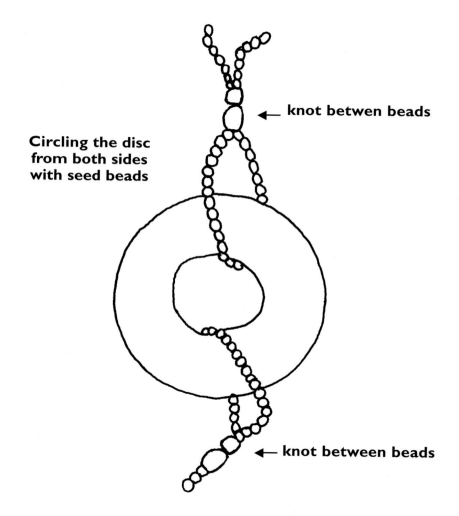

knot betwen beads ←

Circling the disc from both sides with seed beads

←— **knot between beads**

4 Beginning the same way doing the same thing with the other two discs, you now have 6 strands going each direction. String carefully varying your colors and shapes as you string over the intervening discs.

5 When you have strung past the outer discs on each side even up your strands and put all 6 strands through one medium size bead.

6 This is the safest way to pick up your necklace, (hold it just beyond where all the strands are held by the one bead). Go to the mirror and adjust the strands the way you want them and then even up the strands and put them back in the bead on each side that holds them. (The length from holding bead to holding bead is up to you, the holding bead should be under the back of each ear).

7 From the holding bead string each of the six strands, separately or in pairs (you can get two fishline strands in one 10 o seeds) to even lengths. Notice that I switched from charolottes in the front to 10 o in the back. They are the same color seed beads. It takes more time and more beads to string individually and 3 strands look neater than 6 strands. String to desired length.

**6 strands going into bead,
3 coming out the back,
as each has 2 fish line strands**

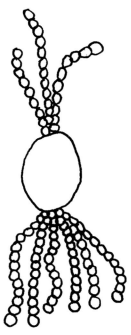

8 Using a beadtip on each pair (2 fishline strands) knot inside and finish with cazy glue on knot and cut flush. You can get 6 lengths of fishline into just one beadtip, knot, glue, close and cut. Attach bead tip to clasp ends. This way you could use a single strand clasp.

ENJOY! This necklace will bring you a lot of attention when you wear it and meanwhile you can be searching for your next trio of interesting and unusual discs to work with.

PROJECT 19
THE CRACKER-JACK LACING NECKLACE

Supplies

- 8-12 stone shapes of the same or corresponding color stone, (they must have openings or holes through them).

- One matching stone, "pi" with an opening that is 1 1/4 inches in diameter, middle hole measures 1/2 inch.

- Two smaller "pi's" of same stone measures 1" diameter, 1/4" opening.

- 12 larger interesting beads in different shapes. These can be either the stone or glass that match color scheme.

- One unusual button with shank back to match the color or feeling of your design (brass, Antique glass, cloisonné, or perhaps same stone).

- One hank of 10 o or 8 o seed beads that contrast with you color stone pieces. Think of brown iris, if no other works. Two strands of fishline must go through them.

- 50 "E" or smaller beads to match your seed beads.

- 12 lb. beading filament (fish line)

Step-By-Step Instructions

1. Cut a length of fishline that is 5 yards or 5 arm lengths long and string on enough seed beads to go around the side of your large stone "pi".

Diagram I
Encircle large "pi" with seed beads

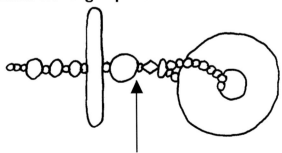

Tie knot and pull it into bigger bead

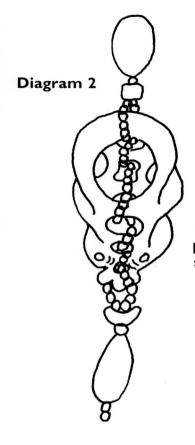

Diagram 2

Lacing in and out of pieces with seed beads

2. Now go through several larger beads with both strands, you can even tie a simple knot (one strand over the other) between these beads to secure your strands. Diagram 2

3. Attach your first carved stone piece by stringing seed beads separately on each strand and lacing (in and out) through the holes or open spaces of the piece. Continue in this same manner, changing the width and configuration of the necklace by the way you add your beads and stone pieces and small pi's. Diagram 2.

4. As you progress fit the necklace around your neck so that the most interesting parts end up where you want them to be. I put the big "Pi" just above my left breast because that is where I want my focal point to be and then work the stone pieces down to the longest in front and then around in a circle. This necklace will not have to go over your head because it has a clasp, therefore it can be shorter.

5. When you get around to the right back part of your neck you can use only smaller beads as it will be more comfortable on the neck to wear. Begin to put some interesting pieces high on your left neck, coming out of the back and string on your button supporting it underneath with an "E" bead on each side of it if necessary, just above the big Pi. Diagram 3 — below.

Diagram 3
Button supported by "E" bead

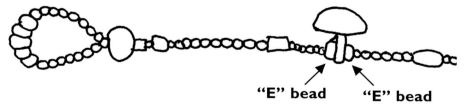

"E" bead   "E" bead

6. Now set up a button loop by coming through the big Pi and clearing it then divide into two separate strands of seeds beads and ending the entire necklace by knotting off fishline between "E" beads in the loop. Crazy glue your knots whenall work is finished, snip tails. Diagram 4 — below.

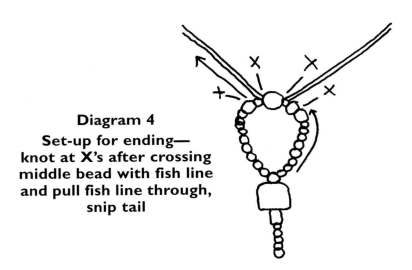

Diagram 4
Set-up for ending—
knot at X's after crossing
middle bead with fish line
and pull fish line through,
snip tail

INSPIRATION

The inspiration for this necklace came from playing with the different shapes and color variations within a particular stone and size of carved pieces. The pieces remind me of animal crackers or the prizes from cracker jacks. I also am a fan of the premise that in some cases more is much more interesting and exciting.....so if a few of these pieces might look good on a necklace, how wonderful and impressive would many of them be! Collect your pieces, some suggestions might be serpentine, ho-chow or brown jade, cornelian, bone, wood or any other material in which there is a variety of carved pieces with holes in them in various sizes and beads that match. Lay them out, rearranging until you are pleased with the way the shapes look in a circle going around the neck and you have enough to make this necklace. The other interesting thing about this necklace is that the design of the hidden closure can be used in other necklace designs as well.

Color Study

SMALL COLOR STUDY

I am including this picture as a small color study. It is a break for the eyes and the mind between projects. I have a very detailed and lengthy color study in my first book and if you have not read it, you should. My innate design sense always starts with color, it is the way I arrange my beads and all other supplies. It is the way I think! All my designing is governed by color and proportion. To me, color is everything!

At first glance these two necklaces look very different, but in truth, the pearls which are the focal point of both came off the same strand which I split in half. Because the pearls were so expensive I immediately decided they would have to work for more than one piece of jewelry. I decided to challenge myself by trying to make the same necklace, using the same pearls, but to make each one look different, using an entirely unique color scheme. You can see how each is very individual.

I suggest, that you set up a similar exercise for yourself. It will teach you a lot about how to use color, as well as how to create a one-of-a-kind piece of jewelry. To expand your use of color, just do it, don't be afraid. If you hate the finished product you can always recycle the beads and elements. I know you will have learned something valuable.

20 Horseshoe and Feather Necklace

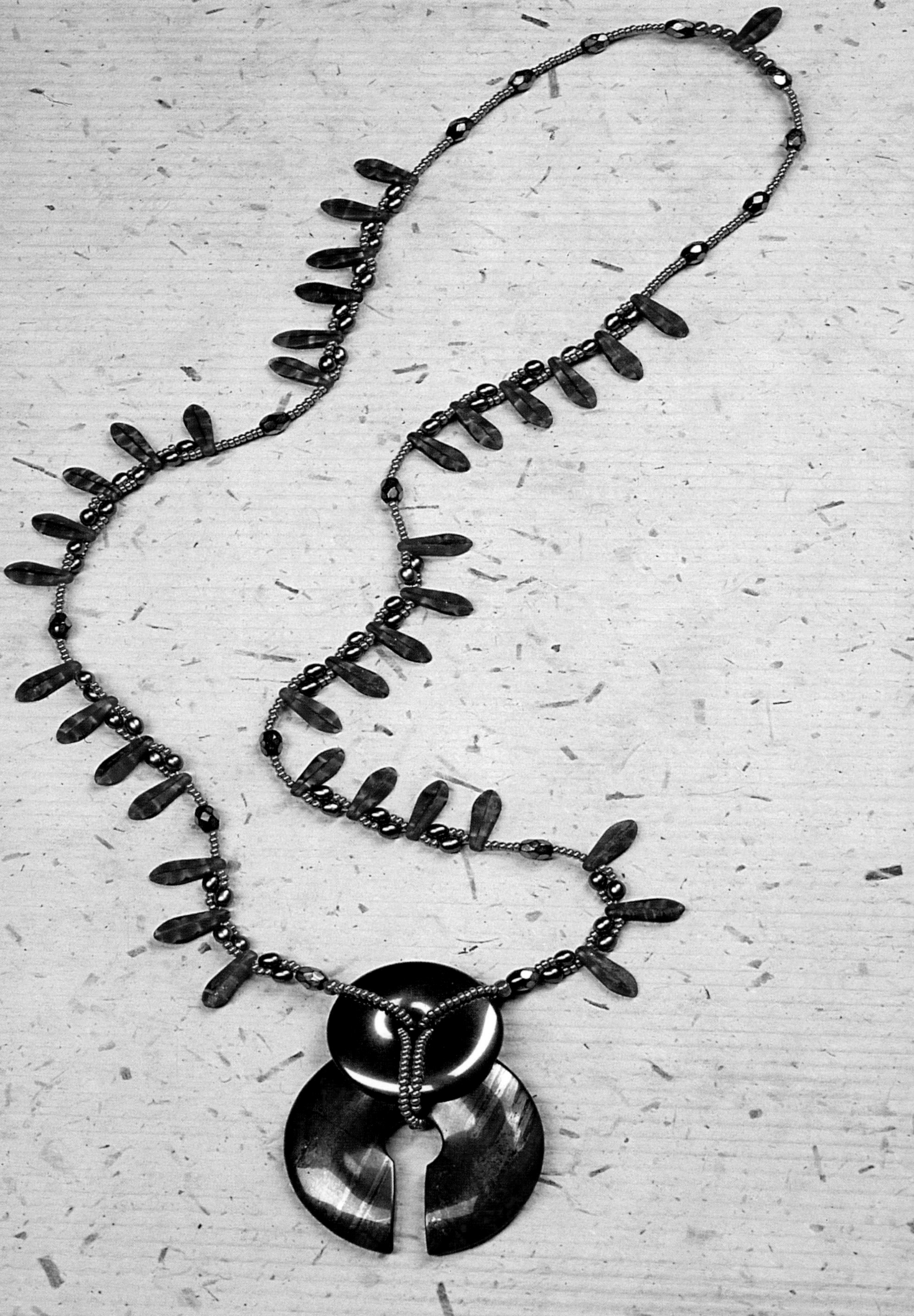

SECTION 6 NEW STRINGING TECHNIQUES

PROJECT 20
HORSESHOE AND FEATHER NECKLACE, USING DOUBLE STRINGING

SECTION 6

Supplies
- 12 lb. fishline
- 1 stone horseshoe shape, 2 inches from top to bottom in direction of slit
- 1 stone "Pi" in coordinating color, 1 1/8th inch in diameter
- 4 loops of size 10 o seed bead
- 12 "E" beads to match seeds
- 40 feather or dagger beads to match color scheme
- 20 6mm beads (I used oval faceted beads, but any shape is fine)
- 60 small pearls with vertical holes (the shape is called "potato or oval, about 4mm in size)

Step-By-Step Instructions

1 Cut 2 strands of fishline 2 yards long each.

2 String on 40 seed beads on each piece of fishline and drop to the middle of each length. You should now be holding 4 ends.

3 Taking one end from each strand put it through the hole of the "pi" from the front to the back, then put the other two ends of the two strands through the hole of the "pi" from the back to the front. It is less confusing if you put the second set of ends either to the outsides or insides of the first two ends. It does not matter which you choose.

4 Now slide your horseshoe shape in the bottom loop of seed beads letting it dangle or hang down and then tighten by putting an "E" bead on each side (each side is a combination of one front strung and one back strung strand that is through "pi") Make a small knot of these 2 strands and then string on a 6mm bead which should fit over the knot.

Diagram #2.

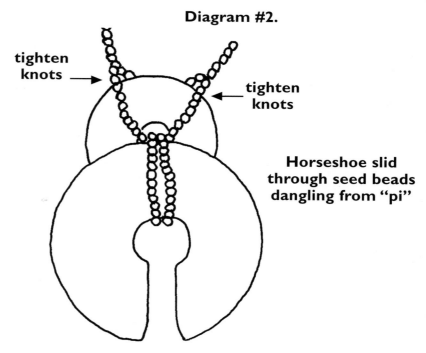

tighten knots →

← **tighten knots**

Horseshoe slid through seed beads dangling from "pi"

5 Now string on a *pearl on one strand and then 3 seed beads and on the other strand the reverse, first 3 seed beads and then a pearl and then string a feather beads on both strands * Repeat from * to * twice more.

Diagram #3.

6 Now string on 5 seed beads on both fishline strands, then one 6mm bead and then another 5 seed beads again. * repeat steps #5 ending with feather or dagger bead and then repeat step #6. (see picture)

7 Repeat steps #5 using 5 feathers and then finish with step #6.

8 Repeat steps #5 using 6 feathers and then finish with step #6.

9 Then string on one 6mm bead with 8 seed beads inbetween on both strands on each side, repeating these beads until you reach the overall length that you desire. Mine is 3 and 1/2 inches from the last feather bead or a total of 17 inches on each side of the necklace, total side length. (34 inches in all or both sides)

10 Now string on 3 "E" beads on each side then one feather bead and cross the strands over, stringing through the feather bead and through 1st "E" bead on the other side. Knot over strands and the same thing again after next "E" bead. Back string into 6mm beads. Crazy glue the knots and cutoff the naked fishline ends flush.

POSTSCRIPT

This makes a simple yet very interesting necklace that has no clasp and fits over your head. This is just one complete necklace that illustrates double stringing which makes simple stringing look very intricate and fuller. It also gives an enthnic look to simple stone pieces. Enjoy!

PROJECT 21
SIDE STRUNG BEAD NECKLACE

Supplies

- 12 lb. fishline
- 1 pendant
- 1 large oval or flat bead
- 1/2 hank or 6 loops of 10 o seed beads
- 1 medium or large bead
- 4 small or medium beads, 2 of which should be flat or oval.
- 2 tusk shells
- Misc. "E" beads and "fancy" beads to match color scheme

Step-By-Step Instructions

1   Cut 2 strands of fishline 2 1/2 yards long each.

2   String on 30 seeds beads or enough to go through hole and around pendant side onto each piece of fishline and put a 4mm or "E" bead on both strand ends (thus 1 long strand of fishline becomes 2). Follow Diagram 1 up from pendent.

3   Now string on 12 seed beads on both strands on each side.

4   Put these same 2 ends into the big flat bead coming in from both sides and coming out the opposite side (the hole of the big bead should be small enough to trap seeds outside of the bead).

5   String on the same number of seed beads on all four strands coming out of the 1 large flat bead and then string all four into a larger or diamond shaped bead.

6   String on equal numbers of seed beads and decorative beads on both strands and then split the 2 strands on each side to string oval or flat beads sideways, then string on medium beads onto both strands and continue to string at random again.

7   String tusk shells on both strands on each side.

8 String seed beads on each strand separately (2 on each side for 7 inches and end with bigger beads hiding knots inside, as in a dangle. This necklace ties on. You can vary the length of the seed bead ties or end with beadtips and a clasp if you wish. The total length of this necklace is 19 inches on each side.

The amount of seed beads may vary in accordance with the pendant and type of beads you are using. The tusk shells are optional to this necklace, the main idea is learning to string beads sideways and using them in your designs. This method of stringing beads can be used in many other design projects. I found my green tusk shells at a shell store. I don't know their proper name. See what YOU can come up with! Enjoy!

A variation using any pendant

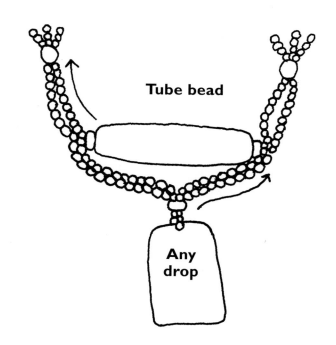

Tube bead

Any drop

Diagram I

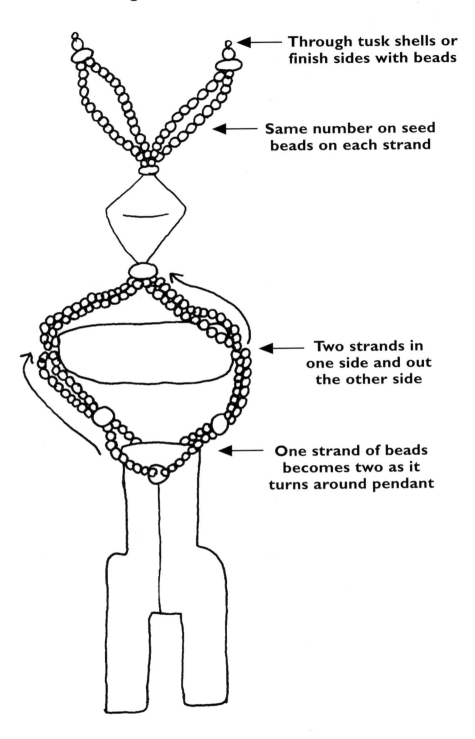

Through tusk shells or finish sides with beads

Same number on seed beads on each strand

Two strands in one side and out the other side

One strand of beads becomes two as it turns around pendant

SECTION 7 ONE NEW BRACELET

PROJECT 22
A DOUBLE BRACELET SPIRAL

Supplies

- Stretch magic jewelry cord, size 1mm in diameter
- Small crimp beads in gold or silver color to match color scheme
- Crazy glue or special glue used for stretch magic (K527)
- Fish line (beading filament)
- An assortment of different shape and size "fancy" beads (I use monochromatic)
- 3 strands of bronze charlottes 13 o
- Various small bronze beads and pearls (4mm and under)
- Pliers, scissors

Diagram I

Spool of Stretch Magic

Strand of fish line to pull end of Stretch Magic through crimp bead when your bracelet length is correct

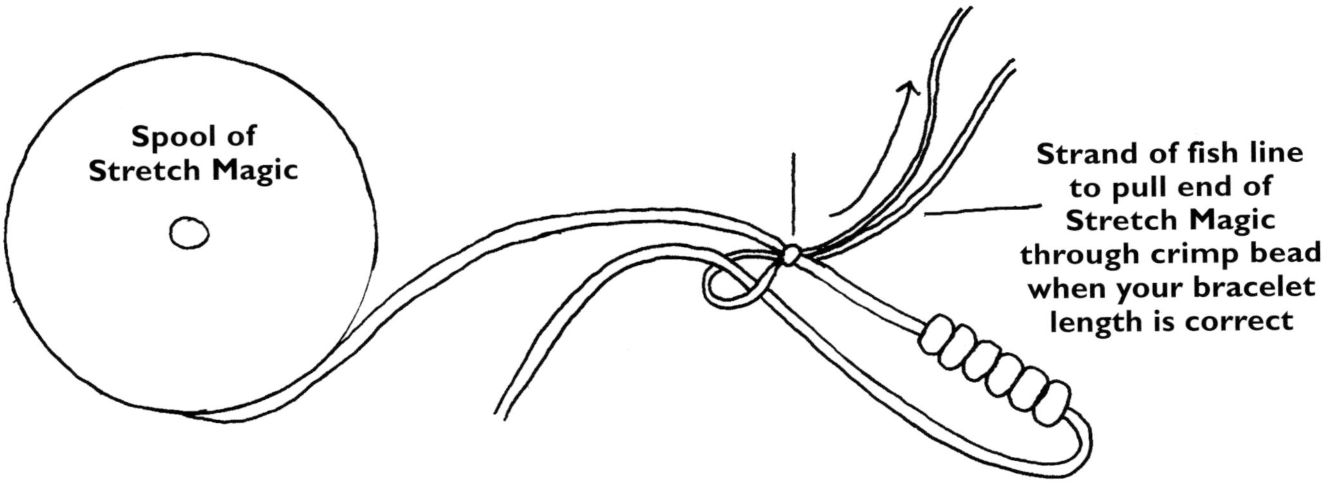

Step-By-Step Instructions

1 Measure your wrist, tightly. Make your bracelet 1 inch bigger and if you like your bracelets loose, hanging down on your wrist make it one and one half inches bigger than your wrist measurement.

2 Now slip one crimp bead onto end of stretch magic on the spool, and start stringing an interesting arrangement of both big and small beads varying the shapes and sizes. Measure and end exactly at your designated length.

3 Now make a stringer out of a length of fishline (8 inches) Diagram 1. Put stringer through crimp bead so loop end of the stringer will pull the opposite end of stretch magic through crimp bead from the opposite direction and cut an inch away.

4 Now crimp tightly using a pliers and put crazy glue on the crimp. When glue is dry trim excess stretch magic to 1/8 of an inch.

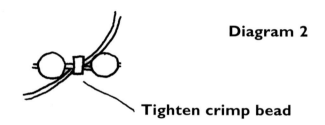

Diagram 2

Tighten crimp bead

Diagram 3
Pull ends of Stretch Magic in opposite directions through crimp bead

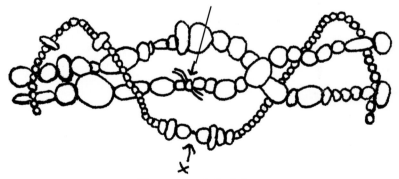

Knot and finish as in crystal rope

5 Repeat this same procedure to make second bracelet of the same exact size and then put one over the other so that bigger beads are over smaller ones and they fit well, but don't get crazy they will work together and can be moved around later.

6 Now take out your spool of beading filament and lace the middle and outside of the two bracelets and start stringing on your bronze charlottes, 13 o, interspersing small fancy beads and pearls every inch or two and at the same time passing the beading filament around and around in a spiral over the two bracelets lacing them together. Don't be concerned if it doubles back on itself, this looks interesting and can be adjusted later if you don't like it.

7 When you get back around to where you began, cut the fishline, leaving about 6 inches of naked fishline on each side. Now make a small bead story one each side (same as the way we ended the continuous crystal rope in beginning project). Tie a square knot in the air and pull until all the fishline down the spiral becomes tightened. This might take pulling the knot apart and retightening if there are naked gaps in the fishline.

8 Knot again between the bead story on each side (same as the continuous crystal rope ending) Diagram 3. you will not be able to get through the charlottes for a second time, don't worry. Cut end off close. Crazy glue the knots and rearrange spiral and bracelets if you like.

INSPIRATION

The inspiration for this sophisticated bracelet was the stretch magic. I like this material, I made a few of the matched sets of "little" bracelets and my students asked me to show them how to make them. The trick of using this material is to make long enough because it does not really stretch that much. The spiraling that holds the two bracelets together is very magical to me and I love it when it doubles back on itself and really looks twisted. Making this bracelet is a way you can use up all the odd beads you might have, combining the different sizes and shapes in a creative way.

SECTION 8 TREASURE NECKLACES
INTRODUCTION TO TREASURE NECKLACES

About twenty years ago, treasure necklaces were becoming all the rage. By description, a treasure necklace is one that has a lot of stuff on it. Now for me, that is not a stretch because the concept of the "gypsy-look" is part of my genes and my heart. Though I dress conservatively, it is partly because I can wear all the jewelry I desire. This often includes many bracelets and more than one necklace at a time, unless it is pins and then I generally wear at least two. I always have one ring on and often more. My earrings rarely change, but they are always either antique or unusual. It is a lot easier and more fun to change jewelry than hair color, dress size, or husbands.

Back to my story! It was about this time that I got a frantic call from a woman I knew who had an eye for the next new thing. She had just returned from a vacation and was most anxious to show me a picture of a necklace that she had seen in a Southwest art gallery. There was no stopping her excitement about this necklace and she insisted I try to copy it. Now it is not my nature to copy others, but I have to admit that I too was fascinated by the concept of this piece. I extracted what I liked about the design and from there created my own interpretation. Basically, it was a five strand necklace with a lot of great charms on it. It seemed very primitive and heavy looking, yet there was that instant hypnotic feeling that a lot of something wonderful can indeed be provocative. The price, quoted below the picture was astounding, even by today's standards.

I decided to change the color, the materials, but most importantly, the proportion. My first attempts were stiff, but my friend thought they were wonderful, bought one and started to take orders. I was a little dumbfounded, but agreeable, because I was still enamored with the idea of refining my concept of this new design. Finally, I found my own formula and the only thing that remained the same as the original picture of the necklace was that it had five strands, although later I did do a version with three strands.

My friend named the necklace "Heaven Can Wait". This was pretty dramatic, but as you can see from the picture, fitting. I later renamed the necklace "The Necklace of a 1000 Delights". I continued to evolve my rendition of this necklace over the next several years, changing the look of it with the availability of wonderful things that I was constantly seeking to use for its creation.

I started by finding three chards that were each about the size of a quarter, though some were rectangle, oval or square in shape. They had to talk to one another, meaning that they had to have some of the same colors. The subject of these chards varied from flowers, fruits, birds, geometric, and the most rare, people. To these three chards I added four silver charms or things that I could make into charms. Originally I found amazing Chinese silver charms that were two sided, say a flower on one side and a bug or fish integrated into the design on the other side. Unfortunately, after a very brief time they became harder to find, so I saved what I had not used because first the prices went up and then they were gone. During the years in which I made this necklace, the pieces I used became more difficult to find and more expensive, so my price for the necklace had to escalate, until finally it became prohibitive to sell and, therefore, to make. No one wanted to pay the price, and my pieces were still less expensive than that of the original one in the picture.

Each necklace had a different and unique color scheme which was dictated by the three silver-framed Chinese chard pieces that I chose to be the focal pieces. These are broken porcelain pieces taken from ancient Chinese pottery. They were then framed in silver with a jump ring and exported out of China in the very first wave of exports about twenty-five years ago. Many of them were as much as one hundred years old. Now these pieces, when you can find them, have a wax stamp on the back of them designating them "antiques".

Each necklace had from 18 to 24 charms on it, a combination of glass, silver, cloisonné, gold-filled, ivory, bone, enameled, wood, jade, lapis, serpentine, rose quartz, or onyx depending on the color scheme, and all had many Chinese antique and silver pieces and a Chinese coin signifying "good luck," which became my signature. In my studio I had a special dish assigned to every different color scheme and each necklace I was working on at any given time. Every time I went out shopping I found a few things and they got relegated to the proper dish. Remember the story about the little old wine maker, well the same policy applied here . . . no necklace was begun until the time was "right" and that meant finding and accumulating all the correct pieces.

The things that I found had to be made into charms because the most engaging thing about the necklace was that every wonderful piece moved. To accomplish this I used one of my silversmithing skills, of making charms from beads and small found objects; and then making them moveable by attaching chain or bending small gauge wire to hold them and then adding jump rings. So before you can literally start stringing this necklace you have to make each wondrous thing into a charm that moves.

It also took me over fourteen hours to make each necklace,, from start to finish. Each necklace had a handwritten card listing all the special things on it, written on handmade batiked paper, made by me, and on the string that held it to the necklace was matching color beads. It remains the most exotic and complete piece of wearable art that I ever explored and developed.

The quest part of this necklace was amazing to me and I came to it happily because I love Oriental things. In fact, I think my love of them is so keen that I probably was Chinese in some past life. I love their art, their design, their flowers, their simplicity and their embellishment, not to mention the food. The process of collecting these precious things was sort of a fulfillment that brought me closer to the romantic vision I keep still of what China might have been like a hundred years ago. Having been there, even in its Westernnization, I did find glimpses of a great and romantic history still in evidence.

This is one of the necklaces on my picture postcards so I know a lot of people have seen it, but I have never written out the instructions for this necklace. I only taught it to a scant dozen advanced students who literally begged me to do so. It took three, two-hour classes for them to make it with much homework to do in between. It cost them between $150-$200 for supplies, depending on the quality and color scheme that they chose. The last one I have, which is for sale, sells for $1000, and like all its predecessors, is truly a collector's piece of wearable art. .

I am going to endeavor to tell you how to make this necklace. All I can say by way of entreating you to make it is that if you are successful, you will never wear it in public without a chorus of comments and compliments. I once brought an entire restaurant to a screeching standstill while every waiter stood around my small table of two investigating and marveling at my neckpiece. I cannot say heaven waited, but I think a few people's dinners got cold!

Before you even contemplate attempting to make this necklace, know that it is the most intricate and expensive necklace in this book! Read all the directions and identify all the supplies and start collecting. I will re-think the process for you and refresh my sight by studying the four different necklaces that are part of my personal collection. Keep in mind there are special supplies you will have to track down and that it will be a time consuming project, but I can promise it will never ever be boring or mundane. Here goes:

PROJECT 23
THE NECKLACE OF A THOUSAND DELIGHTS

Supplies

- Background beads: you will need 145 inches of 4mm stone beads or nine strands of 16 inches each, which is the usual length of stone bead strands. I suggest serpentine, light amethyst, rose quartz, jade, turquoise or any stone that matches your chards which are usually in the pastel tones. If you do not want to spend the money for stone beads you could substitute "E" beads which is what I taught this necklace with, but it will not be quite the same or as precious.

- Either a five hole or three hole sterling silver clasp

- Special fishing line, here is the data on the packaging of mine: Cortland line Company, Cortland, NY 13045. Micron braided casting, 15 lb. stock #mbr15, 100 yd. This is white, but I have found it in black as well so ask, but white will be better for the pastels. I found it at a specialty fishing store and I am sure there are these kinds of stores in every city. The price was $6.48, but this was some years ago. If you are using "E" beads you can use Conso thread #18 in a matching or close color. This is the standard number used in this book and my first book.

- For the stone beads you will need a roll of craft wire 34 gauge, (Labeled: Item #73131-O, Create-a-Craft beading wire, from Sulyn Industries, Inc. 11927 W. Sample Rd. Coral Springs, Florida 33065. Bought at Walmart, Price: $1.49.), from which you will make your beading needles. No wire if using the "E" beads.

- 12-15ft of sterling silver 24gauge wire or silver colored wire from (The Beadery, Craft Products, Hope Valley, R.I. 02832, 30yds, 24G. Product #2490—218. Bought at Walmart, price $2.49.)

- 36 jump rings (add a few extra for practicing)

- One needle nose pliers, and one flat nosed pliers, a wire cutter

- Three porcelain chards that talk to one another and match your stone or "E" background beads about the size of a quarter.

- 4 Antique or reproduction silver charms or pieces to make into charms, not bigger than quarters.

- 13-15 other charms or things you can make into charms that match your color scheme which always consists of two colors pulled from the complimenting colors in the chards. Make one of these colors the color of the background beads and then choose another color that compliments it, such as rose quartz and serpentine; green jade and yellow jade, light amethyst and serpentine, turquoise and rose quartz. (see picture here and a different combination in the gallery section for ideas)

These could be enameled charms, several small glass beads on chain all held by a jump ring, stone rings or small "pi's," scarab beads, Chinese "good luck" coin or any interesting coins you can string, stone hearts, stone animals or carved stone geometric shapes.

- 36 medium 6-10mm stone, silver and glass beads that match your colors.

- 36 small beads 3-5mm, silver, glass or stone for charm trimmings.

- 150 1/8 inch silver, thick, half round wire closed jump rings or one old necklace which has this many on it. This is how we will mark and count out the necklace. Don't get frightened . . . it is easy after the first row. If you cannot find an old necklace, then look for a supplier of half round chain.

Step-By-Step Instructions

I Before we can string this necklace we must first make all our special pieces into charms and add jump rings to all the ones that are already charms so they will be mobile and hang correctly. With your pliers and 24guage sterling silver wire, turn the wire around the charm to attach and close it, add a small colored matching bead up the wire and then turn with pliers to close the top and add jump ring. *If you have never worked with wire, practice and buy extra length of 24g. wire. You will have to practice opening and closing jump rings which takes using two pliers at once, one in each hand.

Diagram I

With a plier in each hand or either side of the opening *twist* to open, *twist* back to close

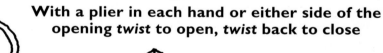

When all your pieces are made into moveable charms you ready to string. Lay them out in front of you trying to balance the colors, shapes and sizes throughout the necklace: the three areas are middle, right side and left side.

Diagram 2

Create a charm:

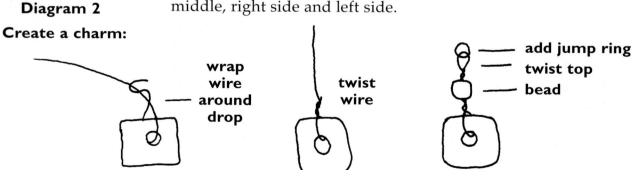

wrap wire around drop

twist wire

add jump ring
twist top
bead

Stringing

This necklace should be worked on a flat surface and not be moved during the stringing process. Each strand fits over or in front of the proceeding one.

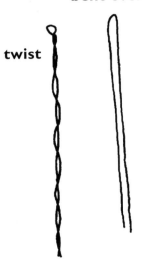

Diagram 3

**Long wire
bent over**

twist

1   Lay out your clasp with the hook side on your left as you look at it on the table in front of you. I am right handed and so I will work this necklace from left to right and when I pick it up to put it on, I will turn it around. Therefore, the left side facing you on the table will be the right side when you wear it.

2   Now if you are using stone beads, you must make yourself a beading needle out of your craft wire. Taking 2 1/2 inches of craft wire, bend it in half, grab ends with needle nose pliers and twist. The reason we make our own needle is that it is strong and the eye will flatten down to get through the small holes of the stone beads. See Diagram 3. When your needle is made thread it onto the first string.

3   Measure out your 5 strands of special fishline at 2 yds each. I keep the remaining ones around my neck or over the arm of my lamp so I won't lose them. Take one strand and leaving about 5-6 inches hanging off the back end, knot it into the furthest left or outside hole of your 3 or 5 hole clasp. Make a double knot to secure strand in hole. See Diagram 4 in side margin.

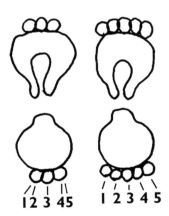

Diagram 4

4   **The first strand:** String on 2 inches of your background beads, approximately twelve beads, the number may very with the use of "E" beads, stick to the measurement. You may have to use your pliers to gently pull twisted wire needle through stone beads the first few times. A flat nosed plier is best here, but if you are only using needle nosed pliers, grasp the wire further down in the wider part of the opening, pull wire through. Now string on a silver divider, then repeat this process two more times, **follow full page stringing diagram (2" of beads, represented by long lines and silver dividers, represented by short horizontal lines).**

5   Now string 2" of beads, silver divider, medium colored bead, divider, 2" beads, silver divider, medium colored bead, silver divider, 2" of beads, silver divider, first Chard, silver, divider, 2" of beads, silver divider, medium colored bead, silver divider, 2" of beads, silver divider, medium colored bead, silver divider, 2" of beads, silver divider, Middle chard, (this should be the biggest one if there is a big difference in size or shape) silver divider . . . this is half of the first strand . . . mirror this side exactly, stringing up the opposite end. This strand must be exact, as all the next four are measured against it. When you are finished, measure

Stringing Diagram

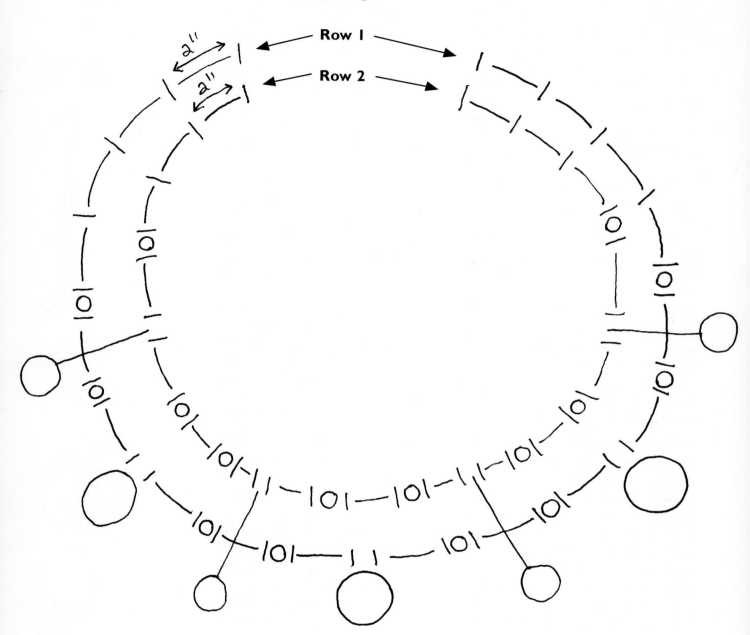

both sides from the middle chard and adjust so they are even, equal in length and side chards hang equal distance from each side. Adjust by adding or taking away the end background beads at either end. Tie the end of the string into the furthest right hole on the other end of the clasp. Hold it up to make sure it looks even. Take a breath. **I will diagram the first and second strands for you. See full page stringing diagram.**

6 **The second strand:** Starting as we did with the first strand, tie a new strand of fishline into the same far left hole of a 3-hole clasp or the next one toward the middle of a 5-hole clasp and put on wire needle. Now string on 2″ of your background bead separated by silver dividers until you get to between the two medium colored beads on the side stop halfway and put on a divider, the first of your four silver charms, then another divider **(there is a silver divider on either side of every bead and every charm)** then 2″ of beads, divider, colored bead, divider, 2″, divider, colored bead, divider, 2″ divider, silver charm, divider, 2″, divider colored bead, divider. You are now half way finished with this strand, so mirror on the opposite side. Hold up this strand in place (hold string over where it will go into clasp) see if all the silver charms are hanging on either sides of the chard pieces. This strand should then be of equal length on either side, adjust and then tie fishline into same hole on 3-hole clasp on the next one in from the outer right toward the middle on a 5-hole clasp.

7 **Third and Fourth strands:** The following two strands #3 and #4 are all begun in the same manner as the first two. Except #3 strand is tied into the middle hole of the 3-hole clasp and the middle hole of the 5-hole clasp. #4 is tied into the closest hole of the 3-hole clasp and the 4th hole closest coming inward of the 5-hole clasp. Now string each of these strands beginning down the side with your two inches of background beads interspersed with bead and remaining charms evenly distributed by color and size on the sides and middle portion of the necklace. Using no less than 3 charms and no more than 5 charms on each strand. Hold up each strand, which should now be hanging in the front of the previous strand, and see if you like where your charms are hanging before you tie the end to the clasp. Tie the fishline into the appropriate hole of the clasp you used on the opposite side of the necklace.

Diagram 5

2 knots around clasp loop, 1 knot around strand attached to clasp loop.
Now gong backwords, back down strand make one knot between each of the last 3 beads and pull tail and through a few more beads, then cut off.

8   **The fifth and final strand:** Begin as we did all the others, in the case of the 3-hole clasp the knot will be sharing the closest hole to the middle with the forth strand, in the 5-hole clasp it will have a hole of its own. In this strand, we will try to fill in any open spaces, while still moving our beads and charms in a balance of size and color. You should always have a charm in the middle of this strand and **you can forget the 2 inch rule in this strand** and merely eyeball the correct placement of the beads and charms.

FINISHING

1   Now that your necklace is completely strung and all the fishline strands are tied temporally into the clasp you can pick it up. Go to the mirror and see if it looks balanced on your breast. If it is not exactly the way you want it now is the time for adjustments. I have a dressmaker's dummy that I use, then I have two hand free to adjust things. The only problem is that she has a 34 inch bust and I have a 42 inch bust so I always try things on my own chest as well. Even if you have to restring part of a strand or move a charm to a different location, take the time to do it now. We are going to knot this off in such a way that you will never be able to open it again and you will forever be looking at what is bothering you right now . . . so fix it. I have had to adjust every single necklace I ever made . . . it is part of the process.

2   Now looking at diagram # 5, knot off each of the ten strings, in the following way: Two knots around the hole of the clasp and one knot around the strand itself, then down through the last bead on the end of the strand, (if you are using stone beads than you will have to pull the fishline through the bead with a pliers) now knot over the strand twice, go through the next bead and knot over the strand again. Do this same process on each of the remaining nine strands. Then I put crazy glue on each of the original knots attached to the clasp. Since the inception of this necklace twenty years ago, I have only fixed one broken strand on one necklace of the fifty or more that I created in that time.

BE REALLY PROUD OF YOURSELF, YOU HAVE CREATED AN OUTSTANDING AND PRECIOUS COLLECTOR'S PIECE OF ART. BE PREPARED FOR A LOT OF ATTENTION WHEN YOU WEAR THIS PIECE OUT. CONGRATULATIONS.

PROJECT 24

SMALL TREASURE CHOKER

On the way to making multi-stranded necklaces with many small beads, I accumulated a lot of larger beads. To me, "larger beads" mean any bead over 8-10mm. Many of these beads were very beautiful and I started thinking about new designs where I might use them.

For years now I have been cutting out pictures of jewelry and clothing designs that I love. Mainly because I am very visual and looking at them made me happy. In the house where I raised my children and lived for eighteen years I had a studio on the third floor. From my desk the view out the window was beautiful and I looked into the tops of all the old trees that lined our block, but the walls inside the room were empty of adornment. I started taping a few of my favorite pictures to the wall and before long I had made wallpaper. It is good to look at inspiring pictures. When I moved from that house I took down my pictures, but I could not bear to throw them away so I trimmed off the yellowed and scotch taped edges and put them in a three hole binder protected in celluloid pages. Now I have started my third such notebook and by cutting off all the extraneous body parts and scenery I have managed to fill every page completely with examples of jewelry and wondrous things. About once a month I add or rearrange some of the pictures and refresh my mind with inspiration. On one such occasion the idea for this small treasure necklace clicked.

After the grand scoop of the Necklace of 1000 Delights, I was looking for something small, lightweight and easy, but still eye catching and I wanted to use all the bigger beads. The premise I used was to make every bead a different shape and size in a monochromatic or coordinated color scheme to go with three select charms. Then hang charms off center on this special, one strand necklace. I wanted to use the big, half-round wire jump rings that I had used for dividers on the big necklace. These are the kind of jump rings that I found on Antique Chinese charms, the look I wanted to create. They could be made into chain, even by a novice or bought from a silversmith or a jeweler's supply catalogue.

When I finally worked out the details I made about a dozen different necklaces, using every available bead, charm and color scheme I could come up with and that was in a month. The first few times I showed them, no one seemed interested in my design and then suddenly it took off and I sold all of them within weeks. I kept my favorite one, which I wear on a jean shirt and it never fails to get attention and comment.

It takes me a while to accumulate enough bigger beads that talk to one another and that go with the charms I find, but it has become a part of my permanent repertoire. Here are some of the possible bead choices: stone, glass, crystal, silver, gold, brass, amber, wood, ceramic in any combination that makes an interesting mix and works well with your charms. So start going through your beads and keep an eye out for three, coordinated charms that will go with your beads or visa versa.

Supplies

- 3 interesting charms that look good together and talk to the big beads.

- 28 larger beads (8mm and over)

- 12 medium beads (5 and 8 mm) that match

- Heavy tigertail or flexwire for stringing

- 24 larger half-round heavy wire jump rings

- 3 bigger regular silver wire jump rings

- 1 silver clasp and 4 crimp beads to match,

- 2 pliers to open and close jump rings. My preference, 1 flat and 1 needle nosed pliers.

Step-By-Step Instructions

1 Make your charms move and dangle by adding jump rings. The half round wire can be turned around a dole and then sawed open, which is difficult, or if you are lucky you can find the half round chain from a jeweler's supply catalogue or at a Gem show. Start looking in advance and buy a few feet of this chain to keep on hand. Now add the correct amount of chain to make your three charms dangle at different and interesting lengths when they are next to one another. This means deciding where to cut the chain so that the final jump ring will let your charm hang in the correct position. The final, larger jump ring will change the position of the charm, so correct this by adding or taking away one link from the chain. Use the same technique to open and close jump rings that we learned in 1000 delights and is diagrammed there. Put a slightly larger jump ring at the top of each charm. If they are ready beforehand you can merely string them on the tigertail or flexwire as you string on the beads; one between each of four beads just off center to the middle of the strand. Or else you can open and close the top jump ring, adding the charm in the proper place after the entire strand is strung, but before it is tightened by closing the second end. It is best to go to the mirror and see how the strand looks on your chest for a more accurate assessment of how the charms look and lay, than merely seeing it flat on the surface where you are working.

2 If you are on a spool of tigertail or flexwire, merely start stringing your beads on until you are pleased with your design. Put the most interesting beads in the middle and up the front sides. You waste less tigertail or flexwire if you can stay directly attached to the roll. If you merely have a length of tigertail or flexwire, put one end of your clasp on with crimp beads (I always use two together) and start stringing. The completed length of this necklace is 18 inches without the clasp, so measure in between. It is meant to fit just under the collar if a jean shirt, but remember, I always wear my collars up, so adjust accordingly.

3 When you are pleased with how everything is arranged, put on the other end of your clasp and tighten by crimping your other two crimp beads in place.

Put it on and run to the mirror to admire your creation. ENJOY!

VARIATIONS

This could also be a wonderful design for handmade beads or beaded beads if you were careful about the proportion. I keep mine in the Oriental or primitive look. It would be great to use some of the bright colored and wonderful African trade beads and pick up the color with lighter weight beads. More primitive beads, such as wood, bone and brass are beautiful on this casual treasure necklace. You could also use the carved wooden and ebony charms made in Bali and Africa.

PROJECT 25

MANDARIN FINGERNAIL NECKLACE

What makes this necklace a treasure is the antique, enameled, Mandarin fingernails. During the Mandarin Dynasty the nobles wore such fingernails indicating that they did not have to work. The ones pictured here are antiques and I used to be able to get them quite readily. Most recently I have been having more trouble finding them, but there are brighter, colored reproductions out there, you will have to look for them.

I originally saw these fingernails on a necklace that a friend and fellow silversmith had made, but they were used in a different way and the necklace was much longer than this one. I was still in the same place of wanting to find designs for large beads and this one came shortly on the heels of the previous design. Keeping to the shorter length I put everything wonderful and of interest in the front center and lesser important beads on the sides. The biggest bead, of most importance, was front and center, literally. In the picture you will see various treasure beads: faceted crystal 20mm or larger, intricate and ancient silver beads and a large toggle or drop, large enameled beads, large amber beads. There are also medium size interesting beads on either side of the biggest one and these could be carved jade or serpentine, cornelian, silver, etc. The main idea here is keep all the beads in their proper place so I had to find beads that would not slip into the largest ends of the fingernails.

The smaller, less significant beads on the back of the sides are old silver prayer beads and they are relatively inexpensive and easy to find. What is interesting about them is that they have small opening on both ends and can therefore be used with seed beads between them. This costs less and uses less silver beads. It is also strung on tigertail and uses crimp beads. You could also use flexwire if you prefer.

Supplies

- 2 matching Mandarin fingernails or reproductions of them
- 1 very large center bead or 3 beads large beads that go together
- 12 small silver prayer beads
- 3 strands of 10 o brown iris seed beads
- 30 inches of tigertail or flexwire
- 4 crimp beads to match silver clasp
- 2 pliers, needle nosed and flat

Step-By-Step Instructions

1   For this one I cut the tigertail or flexwire off the spool, because I am designing from the center out. Cut 30 inches.

2   Place your middle beads in the middle and then your fingernails, with the larger opening side on either side of your large, middle beads.

3   Then string on enough brown iris seed beads to fill up the inside of the fingernails. When you are just clear of the back hole string on your first small silver prayer bead, then 8 brown iris seeds, and repeat this design 3 more times or until you reach the desired length of the necklace you want. My necklace design is meant to be short and measures 17 1/2 inches without the clasp. If you want it longer use a longer length of tigertail to correspond to your desired finished length.

4   End one side with clasp and crimps using two at a time and then pull all the beads tightly to the finished end so there are no gaps and put on the other two crimp beads and then the other end of the clasp and tighten the crimp beads. You can do this by pulling with a flat nosed pliers in one hand and a needle nosed pliers in the other closing the crimp bead. Cut off excess tigertail.

Again this might be a good place to show off your handmade or beaded beads, in the middle. If you make your own beads you can match the colors to those in the fingernails. It will look great on a jean shirt . . . collar up!

SECTION 9

INSPIRATIONAL PICTURE GALLERY & EXPLANATION

SECTION 9

DIFFERENT EXAMPLES AND WHAT PROJECTS THEY RELATE TO IN THIS BOOK

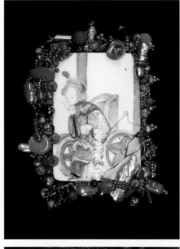

Project 12
Free form found object pin, large 100 year old Chinese chard— "The Rickshaw Lady"

Project 19
Cracker Jack lacing necklace, handmade glass bead by Karen Ovington, bone, horn, shells

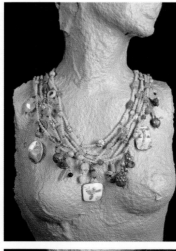

Project 23
Necklace of 1000 Delights, light colored 4mm serpentine background beads with rose quartz

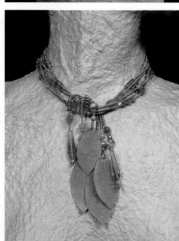

Project 6
Tree branch lariat, copper coverd leaves on ends

Project 21
Side stringing flat stone, rectangles, jade beads and small "pi's"

Project 16
Any bead made into a beaded tassel, constructed bead using jade archer ring and silver beads

Project 12 "Cliff Dividers"
Free form found object necklace, natural shells, raku beads by Stan Roberts, handmade ceramic Faces—Feté of Clay

Project 10
Stick necklace turquoise dividers as bar pin use fishline

"Golden Deco"
Vintage Bakelite pieces,
hand made beads,
amber, bronze, brass,
in the style of Project 19
Handmade beads
by Eleanor David

"Pastel Geometric"
Lariat, handmade ceramic
triangle bead, handmade
Peggy Prielozny snail bead

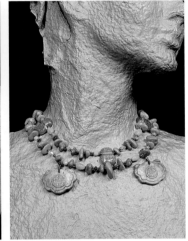

"Made to Match"
Inspired by rutilated quartz,
etched with fish, crystal
and greens to capture
the watery deep.

"Mingled Tourquoise"
Double strand of southwest
tourquoise, handmade beads
by Kathy Wilson with carved
tourquoise from China

"Teal Treasures"
Hidden lock handmade beads
by Peggy Prielozny,
stone beads and "Pi"
Project 19

"Magic"
Handmade spirit bead by
Lewis Wilson, handmade
ceramic beads, stone "Pi"
rutilated quartz

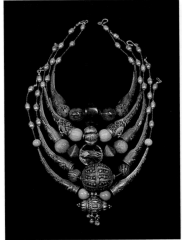

Treasure Necklace
"Mandarin Finger Nails"
many variations of Project 25

"Tutti Fruitti Turquoise"
Carved Chinese tourquoise
pendant with dangling
beaded "tutti fruitti's from
first book bracelet

133

SECTION 10

JUST BEFORE THE ENDING

The best thing about writing and publishing my own books is that no one can tell me when to stop or edit out my words. I think one of the reasons I derive such pleasure from writing is that as a child and adolescent I was not heard, so the words on the page, are the real validation of my voice. In fact, that autobiography I wrote eight years ago, detailing the first nineteen years of my life, was titled, "Voice Lessons".

My good friend Valerie, who reads a large portion of the creative things that I write, says that I often write about the same topics and seem even to repeat myself. Yes, I willingly admit that there are many ideas that fascinate me. In my quest to create a better understanding of these ideas I continually go back to them when new thoughts occur to me.

I think of ideas in two ways. As a tantalizing fruit, that becomes sweeter with each taste, as I consume it. Eventually I suck all the vitality out of it, pushing it out to its inevitable end, yet what grows from that process in my mind becomes the seed of my next thoughts or idea. I also think of ideas as rooms in my mind and I am always going back into them, coming from a new direction. That re-entry, presents a new prospective, because I am arriving each time in a different way: via a window, door, French doors, transom, or even, the small light visible under a closed door. I would go so far as to describe myself as an interior decorator in these rooms, tidying up my ideas. What I am trying to share with you, in these most elaborate metaphors, is the progression of my creative mind, which has a certain chain reaction that gets me to a comfortable, if not final destination.

Before this book ends, while I still have your attention, please indulge me for another page while I make a few more observations. Stringing beads the better part of most days allows me a good deal of time to think. We might even say that my philosophizing is a bi-product of being a solitary beader!

The ideas that roll around in my head are often made clear by external events. Several months ago my sister took me to see a play about motherhood, and while I am well passed the early stages this play depicted, it was a metaphor for creativity itself. I realized the issues are much the same whether producing a baby, a house, a sculpture, or a book. Creative ideas, like babies, take time to germinate. An idea is there within us even before we are aware of it, taking form and growing in our subconscious. Every thought, thereafter, either adds to it or subtracts from it, as our idea evolves.

During the play, as I looked at the audience of mostly women, I realized how innately personal pregnancy and giving birth are. Were the few men in the audience resentful of the process they could not know firsthand? But this morning, while meditating in the shower, it became amazingly clear how all of us are creative creatures, from the making of life to the creation of an entire civilization.

Nowhere is this so apparent as in the Arts. Bringing forth a creation requires discipline, strength of spirit and body, faith and a tenacious, constant level of dedication. This is like sustaining life in your body; knowing that we are the umbilical cord that assists this new entity into the world and helps it to become independent. Think about the poem, the sculpture, the symphony, the house, the business, the computer, the Internet. Every single idea that we have made an integral part of our existence, has been conceived and incubated perhaps by just one person, but brought into existence and maintained by many people contributing to its totality, life and preservation.

My own small creation, the writing of this book, began with every email and handwritten note I received after publishing **THE BEAD AND I,** back in 1997. I realized I had done a good thing, that people liked my ideas and that I was reaching many more students. As I continued my everyday work of designing, I knew I was discovering new and more interesting ways to use the beads and I wanted to share these ideas. Last summer, during one of my yearly psychic readings, I was told the next two years would be particularly strong for my writing and publishing. But still, it was a Christmas card that had come to me out of the universe that proved to be the catalyst to bring me to the point of writing a new bead book.

Whenever I need an answer from beyond my own knowledge, I ask for a sign from the universe and often it comes in the mail. I received a gold metallic card from a company who had done the film work for the first book, whose name I had since lost, sending me season's greetings. I had not had a card from this company since I worked with them in 1996, and here, coming out of the blue, is a greeting, an answer, or perhaps, even an omen. It was once again time to write down all the new things I had learned and wanted to share.

But no one ever really creates anything alone. Without the support of the family, the team and the universe, nurturing and creating become impossible tasks. It was the universe that sent me a message to have faith in myself and the ability to do the work. It is my enthusiasm that sustains all of the people working with me to complete this project. Without all of this, this book would not have been born.

The final idea I would like to share with you is about originality, as it is an idea I continually grapple with. Thoughout my career as a beaded jewelry designer, I have taken very few classes from other people. In the beginning there were no such classes, or bead stores or even, bead societies. I was self taught and self motivated and I still am. Nevertheless, I believe designers, in all mediums, are influenced by everything that comes into their lives. For me, that is everything visual: television, movies, magazines, women on the street or everyone I meet.

Probably the last truly original people were Adam and Eve and everyone else since them, down though time, have been paraphrasing. I even think it is possible that more than one person can think of the same thought, idea or design, totally independent of one another. In any case, the ideas and designs that go through one person's mind and hands, do have an originality and integrity of their own, even if the inspiration for them initially came from another source. This may sound like a huge contradiction, yet I think it makes sense.

THE ENDING

Now that I am at the end, I have a few confessions to make to you. I think I have had this second book in my head almost since I ended the first one. Every time I found some new component, technique or supply or made a wonderful piece of jewelry, I felt I always wanted to share it with my students. But, I was overwhelmed by the entire publishing process and marveled that I had ever pulled it all together on my own the first time. I compare it to looking at my grown children and marveling at having given birth to them and raised them. There is some sort of naivete that gets you through a process you know little about the first time, that evaporates the second time around. I thought writing this new, even bigger book, would just be too difficult. I actually thought of not writing this book....it was going to be too much effort, but then several things happened to make me change my mind.

First of all, I had already written up seven new projects, ones I had promised I would in *The Bead and I.* Second, almost everyone who had helped me with the first book was willing to help me again and thought it was a good idea. Third, during the time I faltered most, the universe sent me signs that this book was meant to be written. As a close friend of mine said to me one day when I was unsure, "Marla, no one but you can write this book." I realized he was right.

And so began the slow process of creating this book. Every day I either actually made or remade a piece of jewelry or wrote up the instructions, first in longhand, and then on the computer. Soon my pile of computer revisions, which were stacked upon the dresser in my bedroom for me to see first thing every morning, began to look impressive. One by one my outline began to fill in, diagrams got drawn, the final pieces got made and put in order to be photographed and arranged. My daily momentum assured me there was no turning back.

Though I make it a point never to say never, I do believe that this will be the last bead book I will write. That is why I have tried to include every possible new idea, technique, design and morsel of advise that I know. As a result, I think this book is more exciting than the last one. In addition, I have paid particular attention to putting it together sequentially, in exactly the way I learned each new step. I did that by first learning the simple use of a new technique or supply and then employing that knowledge to create new designs. I translated many new techniques back and forth from pins to necklaces, or visa-versa, to apply that technique in new interpretations.

I receive a new age monthly magazine in which the editor, in his column entitled "My Current Opinion," gives his often changing opinions on things. I enjoy it because he is aware of the importance of being open to new ideas and of changing one's mind. And although I feel this is my last bead book, there may come a time when I want to share with you again. For now, however, I will be going back to work on my personal philosophy book and categorizing the more than two thousand poems I continue to write. I hope you will look for these books as well.

But for now, I hope you will find this book, informative, enjoyable and challenging; and that you will treasure the pieces you create to adorn your body and others as you bring more beauty into the world.

I am always happy and eager to hear from my readers and students. You may feel free to contact me with any of your questions or comments, by phone, snail mail or Email. Hopefully, we will meet at some wonderful beading conference or retreat and until then, I wish you a sparkling beaded journey.....

You can reach me by e-mail at MGas726@cs.com

You can find my website at www.MGassnerjewelry

You can reach me at the following address and phone number:

Marla L. Gassner

213 Woodstone Drive, Buffalo Grove, Illinois 60089-6703

Phone: (847) 541-1910

There is a good chance I may be moving out of the midwest in the next year, so if you cannot get me at the above address or phone you can e-mail me or contact me through my website: www.mgassnerjewelry.com.

DB